STUDIES IN MODERN EUROPEAN LITERATURE
AND THOUGHT

General Editor:
E R I C H   H E L L E R
Professor of German
in the University College of Swansea

J A C Q U E S   R I V I È R E

*

Also by Martin Turnell

POETRY AND CRISIS

THE CLASSICAL MOMENT
Studies of Corneille, Molière, Racine

THE NOVEL IN FRANCE

JACQUES RIVIÈRE

MARTIN TURNELL

Mes maîtres sont: Descartes, Racine,
Marivaux, Ingres, c'est-à-dire
ceux qui refusent l'ombre

J.R.

CAMBRIDGE

First published in 1953 in the Series
Studies in Modern European Literature and Thought
by Bowes & Bowes Publishers Limited, Cambridge

To

JUANITA

Printed in the Netherlands
by Joh. Enschedé en Zonen, Haarlem

FOREWORD

When Jacques Rivière died of typhoid fever in 1925 at the early age of thirty-eight, European literature was deprived of one of the ablest and most interesting minds of our time. He was known to a small circle of English readers as the distinguished editor of the *Nouvelle Revue Française* and as the author of a number of remarkable critical studies which had appeared in its pages; but the bulk of his work did not appear in book form until after his death and it can safely be said that he has never had the recognition that he deserved in this country. He was one of the most characteristic representatives of contemporary French intellectual life and it is difficult to think of any other modern writer who can contribute more to the understanding of the French mind or explain more clearly the French contribution to civilisation.

His field was a wide one. It included religion and the novel as well as literary and political criticism. Since his death he has become something of a cult in certain circles in France. Pious hands have unearthed and published fragments of theological speculation, a large number of letters and an unfinished novel in addition to his critical essays. All his work bears the impress of a distinguished mind, but it is probable that his literary criticism will be considered his most lasting achievement. It must therefore be a cause for regret that the critic seems to have been largely overshadowed by the theologian, and we may doubt whether the criticism has been fully appreciated on the continent any more than in England and America. 'Rivière', wrote a Belgian author, 'would never have claimed to be regarded as a literary critic'.[*1] Whether he would have claimed to be regarded as a literary critic or not, he seems to me to be one of the most distinguished of all modern French critics and to be at his best a far better critic than Rémy de Gourmont, though he never enjoyed the same influence as that writer. For this reason, I intend to deal more fully in this essay with his criticism than with his other work. I do not wish, however, to minimise the interest of his religious writings or their value as a document. A writer's work must be seen as a whole. We cannot hope to understand him if we pick and choose, and we shall find that the peculiar virtues of Rivière's criticism are only comprehensible in the light of what must be regarded as the limitations of his work as a Christian apologist.

M. T.

---

[*] All notes and translations of passages quoted in the text will be found in the Appendix on pp. 59—62.

CONTENTS

I

Portrait of a Writer

We are not always well informed about the early life of famous writers. The biographer has to make do with a handful of faded photographs, an occasional letter from a schoolboy to his grandmother or fragments of autobiography written down many years after the events; but he seldom has an inside view of his author during the formative years. We have an entertaining collection of photographs of Jacques Rivière: the stilted conventional portrait of the author at the age of two; the family group at the age of fourteen; the twenty-two-year-old fiancé of Isabelle Fournier with curly hair, tiny moustache and high uncomfortable collar; the slightly scruffy-looking Sergeant Rivière at the prisoner-of-war camp; the highly intellectual editor of the *Nouvelle Revue Française*, head propped on hand as he reads the latest masterpiece; and finally Rivière surrounded by Gide, Roger Martin du Gard and Jean Schlumberger at Pontigny in 1923. As we turn over the pages of the album, we pause at the photograph taken in 1922. The sitter faces us. We notice the wide-set eyes, full lips and serious expression. Underneath are the words: 'Mes maîtres sont: Descartes, Racine, Marivaux, Ingres, c'est-à-dire ceux qui refusent l'ombre.' We find ourselves wondering what was going on in that mind, how it all happened. Fortunately there is an answer. The vast correspondence with Henri Alain-Fournier, his future brother-in-law and author of *Le Grand Meaulnes*, and the letters to Claudel, give us an incomparable inside view of his development from his nineteenth to his twenty-eighth year.

Rivière was born at Bordeaux on the 15th July 1886, and was the son of a Professor of Medicine at the University. He met Fournier at the Lycée Lakanal in Paris in 1903 when they were both seventeen. In the long introduction that he wrote for *Miracles*, a posthumous collection of Fournier's poems and stories, he has left us an account of their first meeting and has given us a glimpse of some one who appears very different from the supposedly gentle author of *Meaulnes*.

'Our friendship', he says, 'was not immediate. We became aware of our differences of character before our resemblances.'[2] At seventeen, Fournier was a rowdy, independent youth always at odds with the direction of the lycée and full of schoolboyish pranks. Rivière watched the 'offensives' against the authorities nervously and was slightly shocked by them. The first advances came from Fournier and were not unmixed with *taquineries* and *moqueries*. 'My serious, scrupulous, meticulous nature made him impatient'; and when Rivière found that his desk had been turned upside down, he knew who was the culprit.

The *rapprochement* was caused by a master reading Henri de Régnier's *Tel qu'en songe* aloud to his class at Christmas 1903.

'I looked at Fournier on his bench. He was listening with deep attention. Several times we exchanged glances shining with emotion. At the end of the lesson we made a rush for one another.'[3] 'I do not know', said Rivière, 'whether it is possible to make people who did not *experience* it understand what Symbolism meant to us. It was a spiritual climate, a ravishing place of exile or rather of repatriation, a paradise. All those images and allegories, which today hang for the most part faded and limp, spoke to us, surrounded us, were an ineffable presence for us. We walked through its "terraces", dipped our hands into its "fountains", and the perpetual autumn of its poetry yellowed deliciously the very harvests of our thought.'[4]

It was to be a long enchantment.

In 1905 the two friends were separated. Rivière had failed to pass his examination and was given a scholarship to prepare his *licence* at Bordeaux. Fournier, after a stay in England, returned to Lakanal and the correspondence proper began. It possesses a singular charm. When it opens they are both under the sway of the Symbolists. Francis Jammes, Maeterlinck and Verhaeren are the authors they discuss most frequently, but Laforgue has already begun to dominate Fournier. Pocket money is short. Fournier's parents are not well off and Rivière is too proud to ask anything from his. There are little clubs formed with other school friends whose members take it in turn to buy the *Mercure de France* or 'little reviews' like *L'Ermitage* and *Vers et Prose* which pass from hand to hand. The one whose turn it is to have first read writes to the others telling them what is in the *sommaire* and what contributions seem good. They exercise the same care in the choice of their books. One arranges to buy the new Jammes, the other the new Verhaeren, and they copy out whole poems for one another.

The long dialogue records their changing tastes, the abandonment of old favourites and the discovery of new. Rivière is *bouleversé* by the discovery of Maurice Barrès and there is a long exposition of his theories. Balzac, they agree, is *assommant;* for Rivière, Gide is an *être adorable*. The influence of Barrès gives way to Claudel who seems to Rivière to be 'bien plus grand que Dante'.[5] In spite of their youth, some of the criticisms of writers in the early letters are penetrating. Rivière respects Gourmont, but blames his determination to be original at any price and always to say something different from his predecessors.[6] He is fairer to the Symbolists than he was to be in his later writings and points out that theirs was an attempt to reach 'la réalité intérieure de l'âme déformée et trahie par les mots',[7] while in another letter he remarks that though Mallarmé had a perceptible influence on Claudel it was 'uniquement au point de vue syntaxique'.[8]

Their discussions, however, are not 'bookish'. They are both determined to become writers, and both convinced that they have something to say. Everything they read is looked at from

8

the practical angle. 'What can I learn from it?' they ask: 'what influence will it have on my own writings?' Barrès had taught Rivière to indulge his duality, to love his conflicts and to take pleasure in watching his clearsightedness dissolve his emotions.[9] From the first he is intensely preoccupied with what is going on inside himself and in an early letter puts before himself the ideal of being 'impeccable et compliqué',[10] wondering which authors will help him to realise it.

As we follow them through the vicissitudes of youth—examinations, military service, love affairs, their first appearance in reviews and their religious difficulties—we begin to notice their temperamental differences. Fournier was an artist to his finger tips. His reactions to experience and his descriptions of the French countryside have the same fascination as the best pages of *Meaulnes*. 'Tu as toujours eu de tout une vision première d'une justesse frappante', Rivière says to him in one letter[11]. His own talents, as he gradually realises, are primarily critical. 'I have feared for so long that I shall never be anything but a critic, shall never have any function but to understand . . .'[12] 'Ah!' he writes in another letter, 'combien je suis peu l'homme du premier jet'.[13] Their temperamental differences produced a slight friction which was good for them both and enabled them to develop their particular qualities. 'From every sensation,' writes Fournier, 'you are always in a hurry to extract the idea; from every fact, a conclusion'.[14] And when Rivière observes that he will always remain 'dans les subtilités intermédiaires', he describes very neatly that need to complicate everything which was the cause of most of the difficulties of his life.[15]

Yet the friendship survived and was probably strengthened by the friction. 'I have classified all your letters,' said Rivière in 1907, 'and am now re-reading them in order. *C'est un enchantement.*'[16] It is a view to which we can all subscribe.

The other events of Rivière's life need only be mentioned briefly here. In August 1909 he married Fournier's sister Isabelle. For the next two years he taught in Paris while working for his examinations. He obtained a *diplôme d'études supérieures*, but twice failed to pass the *agrégation*. This made him abandon his intention to teach, and in spite of Claudel's advice he decided to earn his living as a writer. He had been a contributor to a number of reviews including the *Nouvelle Revue Française*, which had been launched by Gide and Schlumberger in 1909, and in 1911 he became its secretary. Fournier was also doing literary journalism in Paris and working on *Le Grand Meaulnes*, which was published in the autumn of 1913. It is interesting to know that in 1910–1911 he became a close friend of Mr T. S. Eliot, who was spending a year at the Sorbonne and who had been even more powerfully influenced by Laforgue than Fournier. He gave Mr Eliot French lessons and took him to see Rivière.[17]

When war broke out Rivière was called up as a sergeant in the

220th, and Fournier as a lieutenant in the 288th Infantry Regiment. They both belonged to the 67th Reserve Division. Rivière was taken prisoner at the battle of Eton on the 24th August 1914, and in September of the same year Fournier was reported missing at St Rémy and never heard of again.

Rivière spent three years as a prisoner of war, first at the camp of Koenigsbrück in Saxony, then at the reprisals camp of Hülsberg at Hanover. While he was a prisoner of war he wrote most of his first novel, his book on the German mind and the lectures and meditations which were published posthumously as *A la Trace de Dieu*.

He attempted to escape, but was recaptured a few miles from the frontier. He was interned for a year in Switzerland and repatriated in 1918. When the *Nouvelle Revue Française* resumed publication in June 1919, he was appointed editor, a post that he held until his death on the 14th February 1925.

II

The Religion of a Writer

I

Rivière grew up during one of the most troubled periods of contemporary spiritual history. It was an age of individualism, scepticism, modernism. There was a widespread assumption that scientific discovery had undermined the foundations of historic Christianity. Science provided the unbeliever with an apparent justification for his unbelief, and among some of the more timid believers it led to attempts to reconcile religion and progress or to express Christian dogmas in terms of modern philosophical systems. Modernism was not, intellectually, very impressive. In spite of its claims to be strictly scientific, it was much more an attitude of mind, a symptom, than a scientific theory. It was not the product of reasoned doubt, but of an unreasoning need of change; a feeling that in an age of progress religion must change—as distinct from 'developing' in Newman's sense—in order to keep pace with the changes that were taking place in other fields. This psychological need of change explains the hostility to dogma and discipline and the way in which French writers dwelt on spiritual 'unrest'. They came to regard faith as a 'temptation' (we shall see that Rivière himself uses the word) precisely because it would have brought a stability and an equilibrium which were alien to their mood.

The same spirit is apparent in the literature of the time. The *culte du moi* of Barrès and Gide was to some extent a reaction against the determinism of Zola and the Naturalists, but in the main it sprang from the Romantic conception of man as 'a reservoir full of possibilities'.[18] It derived most of its force from the spirit of emancipation and revolt which lay behind the scepticism of the age, but it was not at bottom materialist. The raptures of the Barrèsian heroes and Gide's much advertised *ferveur* were evidently substitutes for more orthodox forms of religious ardour.

These vicissitudes are amply reflected in Rivière's work. His religious writings can be divided broadly into two groups. The letters to Claudel and Fournier describe his own difficulties and doubts. He believed that these problems were not merely personal, but were shared by many of his contemporaries. *A la Trace de Dieu* is therefore a new kind of apologetic, an 'Epistle to the Intellectuals', in which he tries to find an antidote to them. The essay called 'De la Foi' is a mixture of autobiography and apologetic and forms a link between the two groups. In discussing them, we must remember that Rivière's training was literary, that his reactions to the problems of his time were much less those of a *thinker* than an *artist*. For this reason, it must be said candidly that they are important not so much as a contribution to apologetics as what the French well call a *témoignage*.

Rivière was brought up in an atmosphere of rigid, unadventurous, middle-class piety. He rebelled against it while still a schoolboy; but though faith was surrendered almost unconsciously he was careful to conceal his defection from his family. In the early letters to Fournier he speaks of religion with an adolescent cynicism, and is dismayed when he hears of the conversion of a writer whom he admires:

> What I hate in Jammes, particularly since he became a Catholic, is that he is satisfied. He gives you the impression that he finds 'all that' good in the same way that you are pleased to find a room in good order. It gives him an air of being all fair words and empty promises, placid, ecclesiastical in the worst sense of the term.[19]

The discovery of Claudel's *Tête d'or* came as an immense shock. Here was a writer whom he admired above all others, who seemed to him to be 'bien plus grand que Dante' and who appeared to be entirely serious about the religion that he himself had abandoned so lightly. A passage in his early essay on Claudel shows how deeply he had been impressed:

> It is no good thinking that we can bring to Claudel a cold admiration! It is not our taste that he thinks about pleasing; he demands our soul so that he can offer it to God. He wants to force our innermost consent. He is determined in spite of ourselves to drag us away from doubt and dilettantism . . . Those who try to escape from him will find the price that they have to pay. His method of presenting the world is so dense, his explanation so forceful . . . so poetically convincing that to reject it is tantamount to plunging into the void. To

11

refuse Claudel's Catholicism is to leave ourselves without any refuge except the void.[20]

Claudel's work made Rivière realise that Catholicism might be something very different and very much more exacting than the stuffy piety of his family. It was the beginning for him of a long and painful inner turmoil in which he seemed to be faced with a choice between dogmatic religion and the 'void'. In February 1907 he decided to write and ask Claudel to help him. He said in his first letter:

> Here I am, twenty years old like anyone else, not particularly happy or unhappy. But I am troubled by an unrest [*inquiétude*], a terrible unrest which has been there all my life and leaves me no peace ... An unrest which brings with it the most voluptuous sensations, but also the sensation of utter despair ... The worst thing of all, the really terrible thing is that though I am torn by this conflict, this continual tension, this sense of revolt, this unrest and dissatisfaction, at bottom I adore them.[21]

The second passages strikes a note which recurs nearly all through the correspondence. The most arresting factor in Rivière's outlook is his spiritual defeatism, his delight in his own weakness: 'I shall never be cured of my illness ... What is so terrible is that I delight in it. It is life itself and my one joy.'[22]

While there was undoubtedly a strong element of self-indulgence on Rivière's part, his problem was a real one, and he describes it with considerable insight. He asks Claudel in another letter:

> But why *the* truth, the unique truth? Why that and not the other truths? Why not innumerable truths to which we can give ourselves in turn? Why refuse myself so many other beautiful things? You see what this means. It is Gide, and you will realise at once how much I am affected by him. But books only corrupt those who are naturally prepared to receive their poison.[23]

There may be an element of boastfulness in the final sentence, but Rivière shows already that he is a good psychologist. His problem was not *logical*, but *psychological*. In describing it as an 'illness' he displays greater insight than his mentor, for it was indeed an affliction of his sensibility.

The arrival of Claudel's first letter threw him into an extraordinary state of anxiety and excitement. In a letter to Fournier he describes himself looking at the envelope for some time without daring to open it. When he did open it, the contents were something of a disappointment. Claudel was warm and friendly and obviously delighted at the prospect of bringing another lost sheep back to the fold; but the case seemed to him to be a very simple one. All that was needed was prayer, confession and communion: 'We shall be at the altar rails together at Whitsun. You must get yourself into the confessional. Poor boy! It's hard, but after all no harder for you than the others. Our friends have gone through with it. *Pas de respect humain*, Jacques Rivière!' [24]

In reading these letters, it is impossible not to feel that Claudel underrated the complexity of the case and that the impatience which he showed from time to time came from the knowledge that his treatment was ill-adapted to this particular 'patient'. 'I am convinced about God', writes Rivière in one of his letters, '. . . I only refuse to prefer God to myself. I do not believe that he demands anything of us except a perfect and integral development of ourselves.'[25] He could hardly have chosen words more likely to irritate Claudel and he drew down on himself a crushing rejoinder: 'On re-reading your letter, I see that you believe in God, but you want a God who is discreet, not troublesome, and comfortably unknowable.'[26]

In another letter, Rivière embarks incautiously on philosophical problems: 'I have never attached and I do not attach any demonstrative value to philosophy. The more I indulge in it, the more inclined I feel to regard it as the most fascinating game I know precisely because it is the most vain.'[27] Rivière's excursions into philosophy nearly brought the correspondence to a close. Claudel wrote:

If I have left your last letter unanswered, it was because our correspondence no longer seemed to me to serve any useful purpose. If I wrote to you, it was in the fraternal hope of doing you some good and not in order to become involved in sterile philosophical controversies for which I have neither the inclination nor the competence. I see that you have emerged from the period of moral crisis through which the best of each generation pass . . . Today you seem to me to be moving in the direction of Renan and Gourmont rather than in mine. I am not the person to whom you need to write an apologia for 'the game'.

It would not perhaps be altogether unfair to suggest that Claudel is decidedly piqued because he sees the fish slipping through the net, but the rest of the passage strikes a different note:

I am not a *bel esprit;* I am a simple, serious man. As an artist, I despise virtuosi and I do not understand practical jokers. The sneer, from Voltaire to Anatole France, has always seemed to me to be the sign of the damned. As soon as a man is possessed by the hatred of God, he is unable to prevent himself from laughing.[28]

The simplicity, solemnity and intolerance of these sentences bring home to us the rugged force of the man which left its impress on Gide as well as on Rivière.[29]

The correspondence sometimes gives the impression of a very protracted duel in which the parties are seldom in contact. Then one of them makes a remark and we realise that something has happened:

> The meeting with you has been a great trouble to me. You have made many of the excuses that I found for my unbelief impossible. I have been deeply shaken by the new way in which in future I am bound to regard Catholicism. Instead of regarding it as a deepening of my wounds, as the perfection of my humility, as an extreme remedy involving the destruction of all confidence and all earthly possessions, you make me see that it is a form of equilibrium which has to be reached, a measure to be grasped, an exact state like health. And if I cannot desire health? If I am too ill and too much in love with my illness to try to be cured?[30]

'You have one great fault', Claudel replied. 'You exaggerate your weakness to yourself.'[31] Rivière had come to realise not merely that his difficulties were not logical, but that he was perfectly capable of making the effort to be 'cured'. His reluctance to do so is explained in a letter written nine months earlier to Fournier:

> When I spoke of 'temptation', it was not a mere play on words. It was because I am perpetually tempted to succumb... Oh, I am not bargaining with God over the little bit of complexity that I am! It is because I should enjoy sacrificing it too much, because it would be too great a deliverance, too natural a solution, that I am suspicious. I cannot believe in the truth of solutions. A thing which appears so satisfying, so perfect an answer, so natural and complete, makes me doubt.[32]

These letters were written in 1909-1910. In 1912 the essay called 'De la Foi' was published in the *Nouvelle Revue Française*. It is in part a spiritual and intellectual stock-taking in which he goes over all the arguments that he had used in the correspondence with Claudel. A eulogy of Catholicism is followed by these words:

> This eulogy of belief ought of course to lead to a profession of faith; but though the sick man knows that health is a good thing, he does not possess the courage to carry out the thousand and one little things which would procure it for him. He has the conviction, but not the desire. He lies in his easy chair from which he can see a corner of the landscape through the window. He has no inclination to move, only to look on . . .

It is the same with the reasons for believing. However decisive they are, they may yet remain without the power to overcome my inertia or a certain pleasure which is too delicious for me to forgo.[33]

It is evident from other passages that Gide has not by any means lost his charm:

> The reasons that lead me to believe, as I examined them, seemed so compelling that I found myself following them to their conclusion. Carried away by them, my mind saw everywhere nothing but evidence and facility. It felt as though it were completely penetrated by Catholic dogma which had become almost a part of it. I was forgetting, however, the secret obstacle that my heart places in the way of conversion.
>
> It is not a logical difficulty; it has nothing to do with reason. It is not a doubt about the truth of Catholicism. It is simply the impossibility of wishing myself other than I am.
>
> Catholicism has an almost unlimited indulgence for our shortcomings . . . but there is one thing on which it insists and which it can never abandon. It insists that we prefer our good actions to our bad ones, that we desire the victory of what is best in us. Now, this is something that I have never been able to feel. I cannot wish myself different. I feel too much surprise, too much delight, too much interest in every feeling that comes to me. I do not think about its quality or its value. It cannot be unwelcome to me. It is there and that is enough.[34]
>
> I am filled with a passion for self-knowledge—perhaps the only passion that is really impious . . . From every day I ask not that it will bring me nearer perfection, but that it will teach me something new about myself. I do not ask that it will make me better than the day before, but that it will show me more clearly than yesterday what I am, that it will put me more decidedly in possession of myself. I demand not progress but information. I do not try to create in myself an ideal being who will be pleasing to God, but simply to find out the truth about myself, to find out exactly what I *am*.[35]

It seems at first as though he is simply re-stating the views that he had already expressed in his letters to Claudel, but it must be remembered that we are dealing with intangibles. When we look at the passages more carefully, we find that there is a scarcely perceptible change of emphasis. Rivière is certainly repeating his previous arguments, but the stress has shifted from the weakness of the believer to the strength and attraction of belief. It is not therefore surprising that the following year he was formally reconciled with the Church. No documents survive to tell us precisely what happened. A good deal can be inferred from *A la Trace de Dieu*, but the opening sentence of that work is the only one that provides a direct explanation:

The first thing of all is to desire the truth whatever it may be. God interests us only if He exists. If He does not exist, what will be the good of having proved it? But if He does exist, what does it matter if we cannot prove it? There must be no forcing. We must not wish for Him to exist at any price ... We must take truth as it appears.[36]

Gide declared roundly that Rivière was never one of his 'disciples', and Claudel has made clear in his Preface to *A la Trace de Dieu* that he was far from sharing all Rivière's theological and philosophical views; but there can be no doubt that the antithesis Gide-Claudel stood for something real in Rivière's mind and that it was largely responsible for the standpoint adopted in his later writings. It stands in a general way for the conflict between Individualism and Authority; but this conflict has deeper implications. Gide was convinced that the individual had the right to exploit his personality without any form of moral restraint in the search for novel experiences and in the pursuit of self-knowledge. The passages that I have quoted from 'De la Foi' show that it was this part of his teaching which had most influenced Rivière. For Rivière's was the familiar difficulty not merely of reconciling the fulness of life with the acceptance of dogmatic religion, but also of accepting the view that dogma is the condition which enables the Christian to have life and have it more abundantly. What is still more interesting for my present purpose is to notice that in spite of his conversion the underlying tension between dogma and experience was never resolved. This was of considerable importance for Rivière's later work and it is a point to which I shall return.

2

In his Preface to *A la Trace de Dieu*—the most important of his religious writings—Claudel observes that Rivière was not a philosopher:

His was one of those minds which appear from time to time to call attention to the very curious situation in which we are living. There is a wall in front of us. Rather than engage in endless discussion about the nature of the materials out of which it is constructed, would it not be better to try to climb it?[37]

This is undoubtedly true. When Rivière tackled purely philosophical problems by philosophical methods, he showed that he was a mere amateur. He was, however, a highly gifted psychologist and his affinities as an apologist are very clearly with Descartes, Pascal and Newman rather than with the Thomists, with the psychologists rather than with the metaphysicians. We remember that in 1907 he had told Claudel that he did not attach any 'demonstrative value to philosophy', and the views expressed in *A la Trace de Dieu* are not less radical:

> There is no genuine science, no certain knowledge except where there is an experience that corresponds to it. Metaphysics has no bearing on experience. Therefore metaphysics is vain. But there exists a religious experience. The Catholic dogmas can be verified by experiment, though in a very different sense than, for example, the laws of chemistry.[38]

This is a statement of a thorough-going religious pragmatism; but if it is a weakness philosophically, it is also the strength of Rivière's personal position. He had a remarkable gift for explaining theological and philosophical concepts in psychological terms, and another passage from *A la Trace de Dieu* sums up his aims:

> Our methods of reasoning become exhausted even more quickly than our ways of feeling. What could be more outmoded than Plato's purely verbal dialectic or even Augustine's theory of memory? And even in scholastic reasoning there is something which will no longer do. Even in the reasoning of Descartes as well. Does it not mean that *reason alone* is never in contact with transcendental truth? We turn in every direction. Reasoning is used up in each of its pure forms in turn. It is only when it is supported by, linked to, intuition that its findings are valid and unchanging. Is it not precisely because reasoning serves only to develop intuition that it is constant in mathematics? Does not the constancy of its power derive from the constancy of intuition?[39]

We are back to Claudel's image of a wall to climb; but if it is a waste of time to discuss the materials out of which the wall is constructed, it is far from being a waste of time to discuss the capacities of the climber. That in fact is what Rivière did. In the section of 'De la Foi' called 'Reasons for Believing', he declares bluntly: 'Not those put forward by Pascal who believed them to be universal and capable of convincing everyone. Under this title I merely claim to describe the movement of my own mind.'[40]

Religion starts as a personal problem. Rivière is not concerned with logical arguments because he does not believe that there are any which are universally valid. He sets out to describe the 'movement' of his own mind, and his success depends almost entirely on the extent to which the movement of his mind is representative and his difficulties common to other people living in the same age. Religious conversion takes on a new meaning. It becomes primarily a matter of psychological adjustment and transformation. Rivière calls his works a confrontation—his word is *rencontre*—between the mentality of the Catholic and 'the modern mind'. An important section of *A la Trace de Dieu* is headed: 'The Mentality of the Christian Seen from Within'. 'It is', he writes, 'because Catholics are inside their doctrine that they construct bridges which are too short for those who are outside.'[41] 'Our subject', he continues, 'is not to prove the truth of the Christian faith, to give reasons for believing this or that dogma. It is simply to penetrate into the interior of the Christian's thought, to show the logical coherence of his point of view[42] . . . Our study is in a sense subjective—a description of the psychology of the Christian, of the fully developed mind in face of the mysteries as defined by the Church.'[43]

The mind, he says, starts from the necessity of explaining the universe because it is impossible to remain in front of it without asking questions about it. The explanation offered by the empirical sciences fails to satisfy us. It ends with a question mark, with a confession of ignorance. Science simply offers a series of hypotheses without any pretence of the finality which the mind demands: 'For myself, I feel that I am in contact with the real only when my mind is in a state of captivity and, as it were, of affliction. For an explanation to weigh with me, it is essential for me to be unable to find any objection to it.'[44]

This finality, he thinks, is caused by an obscure perception of the supernatural:

> I not only find the supernatural at the end of my reasoning and, so to speak, as its conclusion. I see it; it is evident for me. My sight seems to grow accustomed to its obscure light; my eyes perceive its mysterious workings. First it makes me aware of the immutability of my soul. It does not give me proofs, but simply a sensation.[45]

> The imagination is the faculty of the supernatural and puts us into contact with it. I do not say that it invents it—it knows the supernatural. It discerns its rays in the same way that certain photographs reveal the invisible. I want to believe my imagination with the same confidence that I believe my eyes. Why after all should we be provided with useless senses? And can we believe that reality is poorer than our means of apprehending it?[46]

These arguments are developed in *A la Trace de Dieu:*

> As far as the Christian mysteries are concerned, the contrary of what is usually said is the truth. For the Christian, the mysteries are the only propositions which can guarantee the normal functioning of the mind.[47]

> The Christian cannot even think of justifying himself [against the unbeliever]. For his proofs cannot be transposed. In order to become visible to others, they demand a condition that the Christian cannot produce on his own account.[48]

The Church does not make her mysteries an affront to reason—something that has to be believed because it is so absurd, but something that has to be believed because even though it appears to be absurd, it nevertheless turns out to be true as any thoughtful person can see.[49]

These passages show how personal Rivière's approach was. Religion is only true in so far as he feels it to be true, dogma real only in so far as it answers his pragmatic test. The most satisfying explanation of the universe must be accepted as the true one. There is no way of demonstrating the truth of his propositions; there can only be comparisons between different individual experiences.

It is instructive to look at the way in which Rivière applies his method to a concrete case. He is speaking of the dogma of Original Sin:

> You can deny it with words; you can ridicule it; but at night, as he goes to bed, the tired man looks back on his day and recognises a certain lack in everything he has done, a gap between what he has done and what he intended to do. He has spared no pains; until night came he made the same effort and every minute seemed full to overflowing with his work. But now he has the sensation of a sort of failure and he was unable to do anything to avoid it. We apply ourselves in vain. A faint and persistent ill-fortune seems to brood over all our enterprises. We never quite manage to catch up with the thing on which our eyes are fixed. There comes a mysterious moment when the train of thought we are following eludes and escapes us. When we come to the end of our work, it seems to be just ahead of us, mocking us and leaving nothing but its mutilated image in our hands.[50]

I want to suggest that this is the theology of a literary critic. Pragmatism is dangerous in religion, but it is the essential foundation of literary criticism. The literary critic no less than the theologian is dealing with intangibles. He analyses and interprets the experience of a writer as reflected in his own sensibility. He cannot 'prove' that one book is good and another bad; or, to use Rivière's words, 'his proofs cannot be transposed'. He cannot be sure of inducing in the reader his own state of mind. All that he can do is to try to persuade us that an author is worth reading, invite us to enter imaginatively into his experience and agree that his interpretation is 'true'.

That is what I meant when I said at the beginning of this essay that the peculiar virtues of Rivière's criticism are only comprehensible in the light of what seem to me to be the limitations of his work as a Christian apologist. For it was precisely the sensitiveness and the insight of the literary critic which prevented him from being taken in by the religious publicist. He wrote in a letter to Gide:

Like you I have a horror of everything that smacks of apologetics, argumentation, mechanism, construction of proofs, etc.... I have a horror of Chesterton among other reasons because he is a gentlemen who demonstrates. He rolls up his cuffs; he prepares his little apparatus and away he goes to prove that Christianity is the true religion ... Where we see very clearly the ugliness of Chesterton is in the polemical quality of his images. They are not chosen in order to describe, but in order to convince. They are like compères who are brought into the lecture room. They are large and striking like the beams of a search-light and are intended to send a murmur round the audience ... There is an anxiety to hide the faults of the argument, to cover it up where it is false, which is exactly the opposite of my method, because I have not chosen to speak unless I had something to say. Chesterton fills up with deductions all the places where truth withdraws, trying in that way to impress us by the size and importance of his machine. Now I have spoken only where I saw some truth emerge from the immense ocean of uncertainty.[51]

As the comment of a mature mind on the methods of Chesterton this seems to me to be final and unanswerable. It is final and unanswerable because the literary critic has refused to allow the content of the work to blind him to the inherent falsity of the approach and the writer's attempt to bounce us into sharing his convictions. It is here that Rivière had the advantage over Claudel whose admiration for Chesterton is well known. Claudel is extremely effective when dealing with a second-rate anti-clerical like Souday, but criticism like Rivière's of a man whose faith he shares has always lain tantalisingly outside his reach.

Claudel's reputation as a poet is difficult for some of us to understand, but there is no doubt that he played a decisive part in Rivière's development, nor can it fairly be denied that his influence was in the long run a beneficial one. It was beneficial not simply because he convinced Rivière, but because it provided exactly the right sort of corrective to Rivière's extravagances. It would be equally unjust to pretend, as his enemies have done, that Gide's influence was wholly bad. Whatever his shortcomings, it is only right to admit that he developed and preserved Rivière's natural sensitiveness and prevented him from being completely dominated by Claudel's rigid outlook. It was because Rivière was constantly exposed to two contrary forces that the tension between dogma and experience to which I have referred was never resolved. It became an immense asset in his literary criticism and enabled him to work out a new conception of classicism which was much more flexible and much more comprehensive than the theories of men like Lasserre or Massis. For the critic has to realise that whatever his personal beliefs, in literature no order can ever be the final order, that its life and vitality depend on perpetual change. It was because Rivière saw that classicism was not something which happened in the seventeenth century, but a method of apprehending experience which belongs almost as much to Proust as to Racine, that he was saved from the particular snares that lie in wait for the French critic.

It remains for me to comment on another matter of some delicacy. Rivière's apologetic was clearly unsound and it is hardly surprising that his attachment to the Catholic Church was intermittent. This was a source of satisfaction to people who did not like his views and an embarrassment to his friends. I do not propose to stress the personal issues here, but I do want to say something of their general implications. Claudel and Rivière represent contrasted outlooks and they were both very much the product of the religious situation of their time. Claudel clearly belongs to the Thomist camp. Now the revival of Thomism was an attempt by the Church to counteract the philosophical confusion of the nineteenth century, and it stands for an attitude of intransigent opposition to the disruptive tendencies of the age. 'I should not like', said Rivière in a letter to Fournier, 'I should not like to be confused with these "modernists" who turn faith into a form of *inquiétude*, a perpetual recovery after doubt. If I do not believe, it is because I conceive faith as something unalterable and I cannot feel it as such.'[52] In spite of his disclaimer, this passage seems to me to describe Rivière's position and influence very neatly. He stood for an attitude of compromise and his place was really on the side of the Catholic modernists. I find Claudel's rigidity and intolerance excessively unsympathetic and I always suspect that his condemnation of some of France's greatest writers—Stendhal is an example—is motivated by his religious views which blind him to their artistic excellences. This does not mean that Rivière's approach commends itself to me. On the contrary, his influence seems to me to have been deplorable. He was very largely responsible for the cult of *inquiétude* which became fashionable between the wars in French intellectual circles, particularly among converts. He encouraged the lamentable habit of keeping and publishing private diaries in which the ebb and flow of faith was publicly paraded for the edification of friends. It was a sign of weakness and self-indulgence which produced a devitalised, self-centred spirituality which has nothing at all to recommend it.

III

The Politics of a Writer

There are few references to politics in Rivière's early writings. He seems to have taken little serious interest in domestic issues and he never became a party man; but when war broke out he realised that the writer could not stand aloof and could not ignore the great problems on which his existence depended. His approach was naturally determined by his own gifts and by the circumstances in which he was writing. His interest was confined to international politics and for him there was only one real problem. It was the problem of the relations between France and Germany. His most substantial political works are the two books called *L'Allemand* and *Le Français* which were both written while he was a prisoner of war; but he also wrote a pamphlet on the League of Nations while he was interned in Switzerland and later contributed a series of articles on current problems to the *Luxemburger Zeitung* and the *Nouvelle Revue Française*, which have not been reprinted.[53]

Rivière was not what is commonly known as a 'political thinker'. He was not concerned with political forms as such, but with the motives behind political action. 'Nous sommes la grande race psychologique', he once said of the French. He believed that the clue to political problems must be sought in the psychology of the peoples and that a stable Europe could be created only by a radical change of outlook on the part of the nations and not by manipulating political institutions. The sensitiveness and the power of acute psychological analysis which proved an immense asset in his literary criticism make his studies of the French and German minds a contribution of permanent value to the psychology of politics.

L'Allemand is divided into two parts. The first is based on his own observations during his captivity; the second is a study of the German mind as revealed in German writings. The first, as might expected, is much more satisfactory than the second and stood almost alone until the publication of the books of F. W. Foerster, Hermann Rauschning and Sebastian Haffner.

> What angers me more about the German than ravaging, looting, burning and massacring, is that taken all round he amounts to so little. What I can never forgive him is his interior emptiness (*néant intérieur*).[54]

> How little the German in battle resembles the ferocious brute, the beast of prey for which he is usually taken! My recollection of the attack that I had to face is not that of a furious onrush, but of a powerful mechanical operation . . . It must not be thought from what I have said that I am suggesting that the Germans are innocent or that I have the slightest intention of predisposing people in their favour. On the contrary, what intensifies my rage and indignation against them is that they have been able to commit all these abominations with so little hatred in their hearts.[55]

He regards this emotional inertia as the source of their moral weaknesses: 'Such grave emotional inertia cannot fail to have repercussions on the intelligence. The indifference of the heart produces in the German an incapacity to grasp differences of ideas, a weakening of the sense of values. His uniformity appears everywhere; it prevents and clouds discernment.'[56]

This account of 'the ordinary German' has been confirmed by later writers.[57] It is undoubtedly their emptiness and their indifference to the accepted values of civilisation that placed the mass of the German people at the mercy of their leaders and made them a perpetual menace to European peace for seventy-five years, whatever the internal structure of their country.

Rivière then turns his attention to the psychology of the moral opportunist who is always lurking beneath the surface of this unbalanced people, particularly in the political sphere: 'When faced with a clearly defined moral concept, a clearcut situation or a fixed point of view, the German always begins by feeling disconcerted.'[58] This discomfort leads to what Rivière well calls *la morale du possible:*

> There is always an angle from which a given action is possible. If, therefore, you confine yourself to asking in every case whether an action is possible, you always end by finding that in fact it is . . .[59]

> It is convenient at this point to examine the bad faith of the Germans. They can never stand by what they have said or resign themselves to keeping the promises that they have made. They may have made them sincerely, but it was because they had not yet perceived all the *possibilities* which they excluded by doing so . . . Their bad faith is so spontaneous, so innocent; it seems so natural to them to go back on their undertakings that they simply cannot understand the anger of the people who are taken in by such methods.[60]

> They know perfectly well that there is an international code which places certain restrictions on their powers, and they take it into account in so far as infringements are likely to be discovered and to cause scandal. But it never occurs to them that this code is worthy of respect in itself. On the contrary, they are merely concerned to find the point at which it can be infringed without anyone's noticing.[61]

He concludes:

> There is one thing that must be said plainly. The German never lies; he prolongs. He does not go outside truth because for him it has no clear limits. If he goes beyond it, it is without seeing it. To go beyond or to fall short of it is the same thing for him. The only frame with which he comes into contact, where he feels that he is enclosed and to which he must relate his affirmations, is still that of what is possible.[62]

'The German,' Rivière declared proudly, 'cannot stand up to the Frenchman'. The collapse of France before this same German in 1940 cannot be wholly explained in terms of political corruption or lack of preparation. The basic causes must be sought in the national character and it is on this that Rivière throws some light in his book on the Frenchman. *Le Français*[63] was intended as a companion work to *L'Allemand* and was begun as soon as the other book was finished. Unfortunately, Rivière never found time to complete *Le Français*, but he provided sufficient material to enable us to form a very clear impression of the French mentality. The book is nothing less than a national examination of conscience, and the 'grave disorders of our social and political life' which threatened France in 1917 are at bottom the same as those which proved her undoing in 1870 and 1940.

There is one very disturbing thing about *Le Français*. Rivière pays a well deserved tribute to the great qualities of the French intelligence, but he proves conclusively that the French worship of 'thought', of 'logic', of 'ideas', which made possible France's great contributions to civilisation, was also one of the sources of her weaknesses.

Among other things psychological realism is the privilege of the French genius. Nowhere else do we find observation of mind and character so completely free from irrelevant considerations, whether moral, social or utilitarian. Morality itself becomes a psychological factor and, in this sense, the extreme degree of dissolution is perhaps to be found in Racine. It is what Stendhal calls 'the study of the human heart' that constitutes the great value of the classics of the seventeenth century and of all writers who deserve to be called classics . . .[64]

The quickness and force of our intellect are the source of our realism; but they are also the source of our ideology, of the facility with which we become the dupes of ideas and of pure imaginings . . . We have a terrifying faculty of falling in love with ideas, of constructing impressive schemes and believing in them; of transforming our desires into theories and systems. The most dangerous thing of all, as we shall see, is that once they have assumed this form it becomes absolutely impossible to eradicate them . . .[65] Yes, the Frenchman sets too much store by thought, or rather he is too fond of those who give him the sensation of thinking.[66]

Intellectual alertness is a great virtue, but it is only a great virtue when accompanied by prudence and humility. The Frenchman is not always prudent and he is very seldom humble.

It never seems to occur to anyone in France that he may not have the right to speak. No one ever seems to consider whether it would not be better to keep quiet . . . Everybody has something to say, and is determined to say it. Everyone thinks that

24

he has discovered the solution of the gravest problems of the
day; everyone is confident that he has discovered the vices
of our constitution, the basic weaknesses of our social organis-
ation; everyone is aware of the abyss into which we have
fallen 'through not listening to him' . . .[67] The Frenchman
never has any doubts about anything. He never dreams that
he may not be right.[68]

It would be difficult to over-estimate the damage done by
what Rivière calls the *petites voix*. The torrent of destructive
criticism has always been an unsettling factor in French political
life. The refusal to admit that one may be wrong makes true
unity in a time of national emergency virtually impossible, while
the intensity of conviction, instead of being a source of strength,
provokes a hatred which leads the Frenchman in the last resort
to prefer the destruction of his political enemies to victory over
a foreign invader. The story of the two elderly aristocrats who
were discussing the desirability of shooting Blum for 'pinching'
the money levied for building the Maginot Line while the Germans were at the gates of Paris is the symbol of political impotence. In a passage which summarises his thesis Rivière wrote:

> I believe that we have arrived at one of the principal
> causes of our pre-war blindness. When we felt doubts about
> our armaments and our defence measures, how lightly we
> brushed them aside! One or two ingenious and skilfully pre-
> sented reflections on the impossibility of aggression, or the
> prominence given to the value of the precautions that had
> already been taken, were sufficient . . . We know exactly how
> to produce our best qualities at the right moment in order to
> make the most of them. In theory they were adequate to dress all
> wounds and fill in all gaps. *We used ideas to fill in real gaps* and
> we were satisfied. We were calm and absolutely confident. In
> order to conceal the way by which invasion might come, we
> constructed a screen of abstraction; the way was closed, and
> so far as we were concerned the danger no longer existed. The
> defences appeared as firm as if they consisted of trenches built
> of good solid concrete, and we felt completely secure behind
> them.[69]

'We used ideas to fill in real gaps.' There is no need to enlarge
on this devastating criticism, which reads like an account of the
reasons for the break through in 1940. It is, however, worth
while drawing one or two more general conclusions.

It is a mistake to assume that the construction of systems is
a Teutonic monopoly or that German thought since Kant has
had no influence on the Latin mind. Its influence has been at
least as great in France as in other countries and its practical
consequences more serious. It encouraged the Frenchman's love
of abstract speculation, of watertight systems; and it proved

more deadly because it coincided in France with the confusion and upheavals which followed the Revolution.

This draws attention to one of the principal differences between the Anglo-Saxon and the Latin minds. It is generally taken for granted that the unity of thought and action, of the theoretical and the practical orders, is a good thing, and their separation a bad one. The problem, however, is not as simple as it looks. The Anglo-Saxon mind is suspicious of theory, and there is a complete separation between the theoretical and the practical orders. The emphasis, however, is nearly always on practical policy. It is clearly much less dangerous than the French bias towards abstraction, but it leads to the doctrine of compromise and to a political opportunism which can sometimes be very disconcerting. On the other hand, the corrosive influence of German thought, which has been considerable in Britain, has been confined to academic backwaters, and the British have been repeatedly saved from the strange fanatical excesses which have ravaged nearly all other European countries in the past two hundred years. In France, where thought has had an immense influence on conduct, the results, far from being beneficial, have sometimes been disastrous. The more rigorous your logic, the greater the degree of error when your premises are false. The neat formulas of Boileau's *Art poétique* (which Mr T. S. Eliot significantly called 'merely an unfinished analysis'), the aphorisms of the seventeenth-century moralists, the political theorising of Rousseau and the critical system of a Taine cannot be divorced from the facile slogans of the French Revolution, the Dreyfus affair and the theory of the supremacy of the defensive in the last war. They were all products of the same mentality. What needs to be emphasised is that 'the Maginot mind' naturally appears in the country which produced Boileau, the Encyclopaedists and Taine, that it could only have had the consequences which it did have with a people who are as quick to perceive certain facets of the truth and who are as relentless in pushing theory to its extreme conclusions as the French.

The great value of Rivière's study lies in the power of its diagnosis. His constructive criticism is less striking, but it must be remembered that he would probably have expanded this part of his book if he had had an opportunity of finishing it. There is, however, one passage which is important both for its intrinsic merits and for its bearing on Rivière's later work.

The old monarchy is dead and the French Revolution was an irrevocable step—a step which was in keeping with the French tradition. The Revolution, as a political form, died in its turn. It is as dead as the monarchy because it led in its turn to disorder as surely as the monarchy. We need something new, but I am not going to undertake to define it. It must be something in keeping with our national genius, with our tradition, that is to say, something which is in no sense tyrannical, something which protects civilised values and goodwill against laziness and incompetence.[70]

It is not altogether easy to appreciate in what sense the French Revolution was 'in keeping with the French tradition' and 'protected civilised values', but the conception of a national tradition in politics is one that has to be kept constantly in mind when considering contemporary problems. It has always been difficult for the British, particularly for British statesmen, to realise that institutions which have been outstandingly successful in the administration of their own country may not be 'in keeping with the tradition' of other European countries. It seldom occurred to those who spoke glibly of the 'democratic' Germany of the future or extolled the virtues of the Weimar Constitution that democracy in the Anglo-Saxon sense might not be suited to the German genius, and they were greatly surprised to discover that it was precisely the qualities which they admired in the Weimar Constitution which led to the collapse of the Republic in Germany. This blindness was not by any means on one side only. It is one of the paradoxes of an age of extreme nationalism that it has led over and over again to the sacrifice of a truly national heritage. It led Germany to abandon her historic mission as the head of a federation of small states in Europe and to sacrifice it to the monstrous Reich, while a large proportion of Rivière's fellow-countrymen seem disposed to exchange their 'tradition' for a barbarous Asiatic despotism.

These two books are an exposure of the fundamental psychological weaknesses of the French and German outlooks, but the matter could not be allowed to rest there. Diagnosis is vain unless it can propose practical remedies for the ills it uncovers. In his pamphlet on the League of Nations Rivière declared roundly that a *modus vivendi* must be found by France and Germany. He took up the theme again in three articles in the *Nouvelle Revue Française* called 'Notes sur un Événement Politique', 'Les Dangers d'une Politique Conséquente' and 'Pour une Entente Économique avec l'Allemagne'. The first two were written on the occasion of the breakdown of the London and Genoa Conferences of 1921 and 1922, and the third when the Ruhr was occupied by the French in 1923.

The theme of all three articles is the 'psychological disparity' between the two countries and the pressing need to find a way of overcoming it. 'It would be dangerous', he wrote, 'to close our eyes to the vast psychological abyss which is opening beneath the surface and which the divergence of our interests only serves to throw into bolder relief.'[71] The disparity was apparent in their very approach to the issues before them. The French were mainly concerned with the past, with what had happened, while the Germans were for obvious reasons particularly anxious not merely to forget, but to wipe out the past: 'At the start of every

27

conference, the Germans sincerely expect that all the questions at issue between themselves and the Allies shall be treated as a problem and as a problem which is entirely new. The very cast of their minds prevents them from being able to do otherwise. They have a constitutional need of a *tabula rasa*. The juridical turn that we at once give to the discussion completely disconcerts and paralyses them.'[72]

The German pretence that the past never happened, was not real, which was the outcome of *la morale du possible*, naturally came into conflict with the French view that the past was the only form of the real and that reality was unchanging, which in turn was the outcome of the French preoccupation with ideas:

> Our vision of things is too lasting. When you come to think it over carefully, you see that all our qualities and all our faults flow in a double stream from this one trait. The relief given to everything that we express, the bold, convincing character of the whole of our literature come from a mixture of the eternal which automatically becomes part of our perceptions . . . But it is precisely because everything which penetrates into our mind remains there, becomes engraved on it, transforming it into a sort of interior museum, that the time soon comes when there is no longer any room for 'new acquisitions'. Reality, which goes on changing, can no longer find the way to us or a door by which it can enter into us . . .
> As a result of our penetration or rather because of it, there is a continual difference between our mind and reality. We can no longer follow it; we do not make ourselves mentally flexible enough to conform to reality. What has been acquires a hold over us which is impossible to break.[73]

The mental attachment to the past produces what Rivière well defines as a *politique conséquente*: 'We are therefore only capable of one policy, a policy of consequences, by which I mean logical consequences. Our country has been looted—we must therefore be repaid. Our houses have been demolished—they must therefore be rebuilt for us . . .'[74] The Germans may be trying assiduously to wipe out the past, but the French 'are the least forgiving people on earth': 'Our generosity must be sought in the facility with which we embrace great causes and become impassioned over justice, but not in our ability to forgive a wrong done to us . . . In producing the Treaty of Versailles, we have sought a pendant, a counterpoise to the past.'[75]

It is a masterly analysis of a concrete problem in the light of the principles formulated in *Le Français* and *L'Allemand*. It demonstrates conclusively that as long as they preserved their rigid attitudes, the French and Germans could not begin to understand one another. The article closes with an appeal for concessions, for a mental re-adjustment on both sides and the pooling of their best qualities in order to rebuild.

The next article contains some trenchant criticism of the attitude of French statesmen. 'It would be hypocritical', Rivière begins, 'to contest the view that the failure of the Genoa Conference has been a victory for French policy as it is interpreted by the present government. We returned from Genoa, as M. Poincaré did not fail to emphasise in the Chamber, with all our positions intact.'[76]

This is what Rivière meant by 'the dangers of a *politique conséquente*'. The great weakness of the French politicians, he declared, was that they never revealed the slightest desire for any sort of innovation. They had chosen a way which was calculated to please the electorate, but which could only alienate foreign sympathies and prevent the development of a European community without which the French themselves could not live. Their chosen policy was therefore a demonstration of 'the impotence of the purely logical mind to arrive at any fresh conception and to develop it.' 'We behave as though politics were something "purely mental" (*cosa mentale*). We expend unheard of energy in trying to impose on reality a form which is obviously unsuited to it . . We do not know how to study, how to unlearn. We do not possess the patience and the modesty which allow a false idea to disappear when faced with plain experience.'[77]

The implications are clear. German dishonesty and the French habit of using ideas to fill real gaps produce a psychological and political deadlock which cannot be broken except by an 'innovation'. This explains Rivière's interesting treatment of the occupation of the Ruhr in the third article. Although he did not care for it and deplored the attempt to disguise a breach of the treaties as a new interpretation of Article 248 in order to give it an appearance of 'legality', he nevertheless welcomed it as the end of the *politique conséquente*. It was the 'innovation' for which he had been waiting and which might be the means of a fresh approach to the problems facing the two countries. From this point he proceeds with the exposure of the psychological errors of the French which he had begun in the previous articles, and shows the precise way in which the occupation of the Ruhr might be the first step towards collaboration:

The payment of reparations was incumbent on Germany, but instead of compelling the Germans to pay them because they had been beaten, what did we do? We tried to extract from her an admission not merely of her defeat, but of her crime. Instead of starting on the immense task which needed hands, we wanted to start by a moral reformation and a reformation which was impossible. We wanted the motive power of this reformation to be not only remorse, sadness, discontent with oneself, but a remorse, a sadness, a discontent with oneself which did not exist and could not exist, at any rate among the mass of the German people.

That is the 'cloud' on which the Treaty of Versailles was

built. Instead of seeking to discover the state of mind of Germany at the end of the war and exploiting it, whatever it was, in a practical sense, we devised the complication of imposing our own state of mind on the enemy or, better, of imputing it to him and making it the only inducement he had to sweat and rebuild ... It was one of the greatest follies into which idealism had ever led men.[78]

Rivière had charged the Germans with a dishonest and the French with a mistaken attitude towards the past. This led in both cases to a refusal to face the present or, as he preferred to call it, 'the real'; and it was further complicated in the case of the French by a woolly 'idealism'. What was clearly needed was a *psychological shock* capable of producing a fresh outlook: 'Looked at from one angle, and however paradoxical the assertion may appear, the occupation of the Ruhr was a gesture in that direction. It was, with the cessation of all ideology, a slightly brutal but very clear invitation to Germany to collaborate with us.'[79]

He concludes with an ingenious defence of political opportunism on the grounds that it is the only way of arriving at a practical solution of the problem. Idealism must give way to economics:

It seems to me that it will be much easier to justify our action in occupying the Ruhr if we have the courage to declare that we have seized it as a 'pledge' *in the firm intention of securing an economic alliance with Germany*. The vain question of 'reparations' must be frankly put on one side. What we have to do is something very different from rebuilding houses and factories: what we have to do is to lay the foundations of the future.[80]

The views that I have discussed in this chapter have been described by one writer on Rivière as 'the politics of an *honnête homme*'. They are certainly that, but they are a good deal more than that. Rivière may not have been a political thinker in the accepted sense, but insight and decency are by no means the only qualities that we find in his political writings. They seem to me to be informed by a genuine political wisdom, and the events of the past twenty-five years serve to show how right he was on all the major international problems of his time.

IV

The Novelist

1 *Aimée*

A young man comes to Paris from the provinces in order to study for his teacher's diploma. He combines study with some teaching in a school, meets Marthe Villemois, falls in love and marries her. She seems to be the perfect wife, but her very perfection is a source of disappointment to him. François suddenly realises that he does not want to be happy, that he needs tension, unrest, unhappiness. He meets Georges Bourguignon, a slick, fickle young-man-about-town, becomes his intimate friend and because he is weak is heavily influenced by him. Georges announces that he is engaged to Aimée, but cannot make up his mind to marry her because she is too complete in herself, because 'she can so easily do without me'. François is introduced to her and persuades his friend to marry her. The pair do, indeed, embark on what would now be described as a 'progressive' marriage with the proviso that as soon as either of them feels tired of the other the marriage shall be dissolved. François becomes Aimée's 'best friend' and under the cover of friendship carries on a desperate love affair; but the love remains unrequited without so much as a kiss being exchanged. 'You are indispensable to me', remarks Aimée in the closing pages of the novel, but she does not give in. She merely wants François for her best friend. The strain is too much for him. He takes a post in the provinces, merely telling Aimée that he will be away for two months, and returns to his wife.

The theme of Rivière's first novel was not by any means a new one in French fiction.[81] Comparisons with the *Princesse de Clèves* are inevitable, but if the theme is almost identical, the treatment is very different. The Princess is a woman of whom Laclos would have said that 'her defence is good'. Although there is an element of perverseness in her final refusal to marry M. de Nemours, she refuses to give in because she believes firmly in certain principles. The seventeenth-century novel possesses a vitality which is as different as it could well be from the ethos of *Aimée*—the name is a symbol of passiveness—and which is apparent when we compare the opening sentences of the two books:

> La magnificence et la galanterie n'ont jamais paru en France avec tant d'éclat que dans les dernières années du règne de Henri second. Ce prince était galant, bien fait et amoureux: quoique sa passion pour Diane de Poitiers, duchesse de Valentinois, eût commencé il y avait plus de vingt ans, elle n'en était pas moins violente, et il n'en donnait pas des témoignages moins éclatants . . .

> Dès mon enfance, les femmes furent pour moi un objet de véritable adoration. Avant même que je fusse capable de les désirer, leur regard, leur démarche, les tendres lignes de leur corps me donnaient un trouble informe et délicieux, où je m'abîmais tout entier et passionnément.[82]

In the *Princesse de Clèves* we are aware from the first that the characters are social beings who belong to a stable, or apparently stable, society which is governed by definite standards. They may transgress the accepted rules of conduct, but they are never for a moment blind to them. Their attitude to experience is positive and not negative. They do not drift passively into *liaisons;* they love on the grand scale; their passions are violent; they have an object outside themselves and they give 'témoignages . . . éclatants'. As soon as we begin to read *Aimée,* we are conscious that the narrator is an isolated individual; that he is weak; that, incapable of *action,* he lives in a continual *state* of prostration before Aimée. He is not interested in women themselves, but in the emotions they arouse in him or rather in their impact on his sensibility: '. . . leur regard, leur démarche, les tendres lignes de leur corps me donnaient un trouble informe et délicieux, où je m'abîmais tout entier et passionnément'. The passage goes on: 'Je ne me sentais pas du tout précipité vers elles. Au contraire, elles m'apparaissaient comme sacrées, comme interdites. J'eusse frémi de les approcher. Les mouvements qui s'élevaient en moi à leur vue étaient si violents, si divers, si tumultueux qu'ils se détruisaient les uns les autres et me laissaient sur place.'[83] His feelings do not issue in action. They simply generate other feelings which not only inhibit action, but are mutually destructive.

Mme de la Fayette's vocabulary was extremely limited, but it is impossible not to admire the vigour and clarity of words like *galant, amoureux* and *passion* or to compare them with Rivière's strangely blurred 'trouble informe et délicieux' or the Narcissistic 'je m'abîmais tout entier et passionnément'.

These differences were not the result of some sudden change. I have said that the theme of the unyielding heroine is an old one in French fiction. Laclos used it in the *Liaisons dangereuses,* and once again the issues are clear if the motives of one of the protagonists have undergone a change. Fromentin used it in *Dominique* and it is in this book that we become aware of an alteration in direction. For Dominique is a product of the Romantic aftermath. He is the weak young man who does not dare. If Rivière's François has affinities with Fromentin's Dominique, his affinities with Villiers' Axël are still more pronounced. Nor are these the only influences at work. The novel is dedicated to 'Marcel Proust, grand peintre de l'amour', and certainly it could scarcely have been written without the example of that master. But the influence of Gide is even more pronounced. On the second page we find a sentence which is almost a pastiche of certain stylistic devices of Gide, and on the third we find Rivière using the word *attente* in the peculiarly Gidian sense of sexual expectancy. Gide's influence, however, goes far deeper than occasional echoes. In a note on Raymond Radiguet, which first appeared in the *Nouvelle Revue Française,* Rivière commended him for 'reminding us of the importance and the grandeur of normal feelings'; but in the same note he also pays tribute to Proust and Gide for having integrated 'l'aberrant dans

' humain'. He goes on to say that 'in psychology I shall always set the greatest store by discovery, however hideous the object, provided that the discovery is genuine and does not simply move us to stupefaction, but also convinces us'.[84]

The truth is that *Aimée* is a highly talented Gidian exercise the latent implications of which are in some ways more startling than anything in Gide. The pattern of the book is not difficult to discover. This is a description of François' relations with his wife:

> Je ne puis assez dire combien Marthe me reposa, me fortifia, me corrigea. Comme on améliore par des travaux le régime d'un torrent, je pus croire un instant qu'elle réussirait à normaliser ma sensibilité, à en drainer ensemble les élans, les espoirs, les exigences...
>
> Mais je n'étais pas assez équilibré, assez normal pour qu'un tel contentement pût durer en moi dans sa perfection. Pur de tout vice, j'étais pourtant affligé d'une perversité d'ordre psychologique qui le rendait fatalement précaire.
>
> Comment définir cette perversité?—Je n'aimais pas le bonheur.
>
> Est-ce bien cela? Mieux vaut dire: j'aimais trop mon coeur, j'aimais tout ce qu'il inventait de sentir. Je croyais trop en lui; j'attendais trop curieusement ses modifications; je désirais trop qu'il en subît.[85]

This explains the attraction of Aimée: 'Ses yeux! C'est à quoi je la reconnaissais toujours; ils me parlaient en silence de la perversion qui nous réunissait.'[86] Finally, there is his conception of love: 'Je le sentais en moi, à l'avance, comme une sorte d'immense faiblesse, d'écroulement virtuel de toute ma personnalité.'[87]

The triangle François-Marthe-Aimée stands very clearly for Weakness-Normality-Perversity. François is the weak man who is caught between two people who are both stronger than himself. He is exposed to pressure coming from opposite directions. Marthe appeals to all that is sound in him, and Aimée to all that is perverse. This tug-of-war is reflected in the language of the book. Words suggesting strength, normality and solidity are pitted against others suggesting weakness, perversity and collapse which insidiously undermine them: 'Marthe me reposa, me *fortifia*, me *corrigea*'... 'une sorte d'immense *faiblesse*, d'*écroulement* virtuel de toute ma personnalité'... 'je pus croire un instant qu'elle réussirait à *normaliser* ma sensibilité'... 'j'étais pourtant affligé d'une *perversité* d'ordre psychologique qui le rendait fatalement *précaire*'... 'la *perversion* qui nous réunissait.'

François' perversity is more an affliction of the sensibility than of the mind. He does not want to be happy because happiness is static and he is fatally attracted by change: 'j'aimais trop mon coeur, j'aimais tout ce qu'il inventait de sentir... j'attendais trop curieusement ses modifications.' All these 'modifications' militate against Marthe's attempts to impose a pattern, to 'normalise'

33

his sensibility, and in this way contribute to the process of dissolution. It is well described in his account of his jealousy. Jealousy, he says, makes some men spring to their feet ready to kill: '. . . mine at once became something secret and corrosive, like all my feelings. It entered into me like a poison, withering the very fibres of my being on the way, filling me with a sense of death and sterility.' It is part of his perversity that the process fills him with a feeling of excitement, with a longing for the final crash: 'Il me semblait être enfin sur le bord de cette bienheureuse catastrophe dont j'avais si longtemps rêvé.'[88]

In short, the narrator-novelist is a willing victim of the Gidian oscillation, the professional *tourmenté* for whom the certitudes of faith are a temptation and whom we have already met in the writings of the Christian apologist.

The character of Marthe appears at first to be faintly drawn, but this is essential to the pattern of the book. She is less a wife than the sister-figure and as such François' one remaining link with normality. I have called it a tug-of-war, and it does record François' movement away from Marthe in the direction of Aimée. Yet Marthe is always there in the background providing a standard by which his feelings for Aimée are judged. Then, at the close, normality in her person asserts its claims and the affair with Aimée collapses.

'J'aimais trop mon coeur'. It is characteristic of both François and Aimée that their attention is concentrated not on one another, but on their own emotions. They regard one another as *instruments* which will enable them to make discoveries about themselves certainly, but which will also procure new and perverse emotions. That is why each finds the other 'indispensable'. This Narcissistic concentration on the self recurs all through the book. François speaks of 'un certain mauvais fond de mon âme qui n'aspirait qu'à être intrigué, éconduit, désespéré'. 'Il me fallait à tout prix un être différent, étranger, qui fît obstacle à mon coeur; il me fallait quelqu'un qui ne m'écoutât point, qui ne m'exauçât point.'[89]

While we can scarcely admire the sentiments expressed, we cannot fail to admire the subtlety of the expression. Rivière was a child of his age in his desire for change at any price, in his masochistic wish to be hurt, in his fatalistic waiting for the *bienheureuse catastrophe* which would wreck not simply his own happiness but that of his devoted wife. He was even more a child of his age in his intense preoccupation with personal feelings in all their subtlety and in that intense self-consciousness which was manifested in Proust, but which dominated European literature for the first thirty years of the century. He may have cultivated his feelings, but they are genuinely complicated and the analysis is pushed into the finest shades and differences. 'Intrigué, éconduit, désespéré'—we have at once the fascinated preoccupation with new feelings as such, the desire for an obstacle and the desire for unhappiness.

34

This excessive subtlety, however, is also the source of one of the main weaknesses of the novel. Although François imagines that he is desperately in love with Aimée, although he plans her 'downfall' with the care of an eighteenth-century roué, there is a world of difference between the aims of the eighteenth-century seducer and the amorous intellectual of the twentieth century. The aim of the eighteenth-century seducer was to carry the position, to bring the siege to a victorious conclusion and then, after enjoying the fruits, which did not greatly differ from one affair to another, to go on to fresh conquests. He concentrated on the skill with which the physical seduction was accomplished and the degree of mutual pleasure which followed. Valmont in the *Liaisons dangereuses* writes proudly to Mme de Merteuil of one of his successes: 'Since I am without vanity I will not dwell on the details of the night; but you know me and I was satisfied with myself.' When François prepares for an encounter with Aimée he has no hope and no real desire for a physical connection; he is simply 'intrigued' and excited by the feelings which it will generate:

> Je ne lui apprenais rien encore; je laissais se prolonger le plus longtemps possible cette délicieuse ignorance où elle était de la symétrie secrète de nos âmes; je voulais être seul quelque temps à savoir. . . Je plongeais dans son âme, j'y voyais ce que je savais être dans la mienne: le goût effréné du sentiment et de ses modulations, le besoin d'être sans cesse un autre, l'abandon sans réserve ni repentir à la main secrète qui dispose toujours nouvellement de notre coeur.[90]

Where Valmont prides himself on the skill of his performance on the *ottomane*—that strange, uncomfortable piece of furniture to which Laclos' characters were so addicted—Rivière's couple dwell on 'the perfection of their feelings'[91]; where Laclos' congratulate themselves and one another on being, physically, so well matched, Rivière's speak of 'the secret symmetry of their souls'. For the eighteenth-century what was conventionally termed 'vice' was simply a means used by rogues to procure pleasure through the downfall of innocent victims or the complicity of a friendly 'enemy'; for Rivière it becomes a quality of feeling which is interesting because it is 'vitiated' or abnormal: 'Once again I had touched her soul deliciously vitiated by disinterestedness. . . Without intending to do so I had succeeded in making her jealous. Jealous of what? Of the very sentiment that I felt for her.'

The subjective approach is pushed to such lengths that even a common sentiment like jealousy is deprived of an object. For jealousy is normally a stimulant to action, driving the person who experiences it either to attack a 'rival' or make a final assault on his 'prey'. Aimée's, however, is different. When François tells her that she is one of 'Nature's most marvellous successes', she becomes jealous of his admiration precisely because for a moment her attention is divided between that admiration and her own delighted contemplation of 'the perfection of her feelings'.

The truth is that the last thing François wants is for Aimée's defences to fall. If they did, he would experience a happiness as perfect and as unsatisfying as his marriage to Marthe. The game would be spoilt and there would be nothing left for him to do but to start all over again with someone else, supposing that he had the good luck to discover another woman as perverse as Aimée. Their one aim is to keep the game going and they can only do this by concentrating on knowledge—the pair of them would obviously be quite hopeless on the *ottomane*—because knowledge and the 'modulations of feeling' are unending. They therefore remain locked in their strange, static, mental duel. It is the strength and weakness of the book. For we cannot avoid the feeling that it is after all too *voulu*. The feelings are not generated spontaneously by the friction of the characters on one another. We have the impression that the novelist is manipulating the characters certainly, that he is himself playing both François' and Aimée's roles; but we have an even stronger impression of watching a man playing a game of chess against himself and knowing each time he moves a piece on one side which piece he will move on the other. That is why the duel is a static one which can only end in stalemate.

'Rivière cherche sans cesse à se caresser dans autrui', said Gide.[92] It was not perhaps a kind remark from a novelist who was if possible even more self-centred than Rivière, but it does illuminate what might be called the *sujet profond* of *Aimée*. François and Aimée are both prisoners entirely preoccupied with what is going on inside themselves and the pleasure they derive from it. And they are both in a peculiar way *voyeurs* detached from one another and content to watch one another's pleasure.

2 *Florence*

Rivière's only other work of fiction was written in 1923-4 and was left unfinished. In her Preface to *Florence*, Mme Isabelle Rivière tells us that on his death-bed her husband forbade her to publish the novel 'because it would mislead people, because I don't want them to think it's about me and take it for my last word'. When she protested, he relented and agreed to its being published 'much later, after everything else'. It eventually appeared in 1935, ten years after his death.[93]

It is an account of the *liaison* between a wealthy young man named Pierre D. and Florence, a woman with the sexual appetite of Mrs Bloom but without her magnificent vitality. Their love grows out of a chance meeting at a seaside hotel—Pierre is virtually 'picked up' by Florence—and continues in Paris. Married to a husband who no longer loves her, who is apathetic and sexually cold, Florence seeks consolation whenever and wherever she can. On returning to Paris, Pierre discovers that she already has at least one other lover. Here the perverse element enters. Pierre loves Florence, but for a time is prepared to share her with another. Florence herself is unable to choose definitely between the two. The rival apparently provides greater physical satisfaction but Pierre—it is the perverse note again—fills some 'moral' need. He has a solidity which saves Florence from complete spiritual and emotional disintegration. But the double *liaison* proves too much for her and the problem is solved, in so far as it is soluble, by Pierre's withdrawing to his country estate. At this point the book breaks off, but we gather that there might have been a conversion which would have given the whole novel a religious ethos.

In her Preface Mme Rivière has a number of things to say which to a large extent forestall possible criticisms of the book. We have to remember that it was unfinished and that it would certainly have been very different had Rivière lived to complete it. We are told that he did not correct his work, but rewrote it. This prepares us for the statement that 'the artistic side of *Florence* was still to be done. . . In spite of all his efforts to be concrete, Jacques had simply succeeded in portraying a psychological situation, in solving a moral problem.'

It is less easy to accept Mme Rivière's statement that the novel is not 'autobiographical', and we cannot avoid the suspicion that on this score both she and her husband displayed too much anxiety to be convincing.[94] She seems, unwittingly, to provide a key to its interpretation when she remarks that 'Jacques was resolutely working in this book in a field outside his gifts, in a field which was alien to him'. On the surface, indeed, *Florence* appears very different from *Aimée* and there is little evidence of the direct influence of Proust and Gide. There is a determined attempt to move away from the excessive cerebration of the earlier novel and a tremendous emphasis on physical relations. We must not, however, be misled by this. The book is both autobiographical and a portrait of the novelist. Rivière, as a distinguished French critic once put it to the present writer, discovered things about himself in his late thirties that he should have discovered when he was twenty, and he tries to disguise the situation by attributing them to a very young and inexperienced man. The true theme of the novel is the sudden infatuation of a man of mature years for a highly sexed and highly neurotic woman who is his intellectual inferior. This accounts for the artistic uncertainty of Rivière's handling of Pierre and also for descriptions of the sexual connection which might have come from a popular novel:

> Pierre was thoughtful. He saw again the crazy face among the sheets. He heard the cries that she had smothered in the pillow and the grinding of her clenched jaws. Once again he found himself carried aloft by the siren, at the mercy of her tossing, shaken by the tide of her pleasure. Oh! the abandonment to a frenzy which he himself was producing. . . Whether she was

willing or in a state of revolt, Florence's inferiority to the man excited him frightfully. His excitement was translated by his imagination into physical terms. He saw her underneath him.

Rivière, we have been told, 'was working in a field which was alien to him'. The conflict that he describes is not primarily a conflict between two people, but between excessive cerebration and a desire to submerge oneself in the purely instinctual life: 'The reader is asked again not to be too surprised at so much ingenuousness in our hero. We must understand its nature. It was in no sense silliness. On the contrary, it was perhaps primarily and essentially the result of too powerful an intelligence. . . No, the truth is that though his heart experienced a powerful attraction, it did not escape from the immense control of his mind. . . He must challenge Florence's remark: "We are cerebrals"'.

The novel, indeed, records the gradual ascendancy of mind over body, a movement away from the simple, violent physical attraction with which it opens towards the mental and psychological entanglements described in *Aimée*. 'Florence', we are told, 'Florence had aroused his desire, but had not captivated his mind. . . He was still thinking: "The pleasure that one experiences is nothing compared to the pleasure one gives".'

The 'prey' is not so much a person whom we love as an object on which we experiment, voluptuously watching its reactions. In the closing pages, the book ceases to be a novel and becomes partly a clinical study of a case and partly a psychological game in which the novelist enters the scene in order to demonstrate the inaccuracy of his characters' self-analysis: 'If Pierre disturbs her, it is not for any of the reasons that she has just been examining. . . He disturbs her because she does not know how to verify her opinion of him. Her liaison with him is like a sum which she thinks is added up correctly, but whose correctness cannot be proved.'

In other words, it is Pierre's intelligence again. She cannot explain his hold over her; he somehow eludes her, does not fit into the usual categories. But the 'moral' hold ends by destroying desire: 'Serge already in a sense, but above all Pierre, are people who save her from casual affairs, who protect her against the blind and, as it were, impersonal release of desire, but they do so much more by their ascendancy over her than by their charm. They are the ones whom she really loves and to whom everything that is really human in her clings; but what they give her is no longer desire; it is peace.'

It was not for nothing that Marivaux was one of Rivière's favourite writers. At his best Marivaux was a great comic dramatist, but he never altogether escaped that psychological preciosity which has long been the weakness of *la grande race psychologique*. So it is in this book. The excessive cerebration which prevented Pierre from being a satisfactory lover also prevented his creator from writing a satisfactory novel.

'Jacques', said Mme Rivière in her Preface, 'was not a novelist'. I do not think that anyone who has studied *Aimée* and *Florence* impartially will feel disposed to contest this judgement, but it is not a reason for underrating the interest of his essays in fiction. France, we know, is a country in which men have always been interested not merely in ideas, but in psychology. It is also a country in which they are taught to write. That is why a man of letters, with a feeling for language but without genuine creative ability, can and does turn out work which looks very like a novel, and why France is the home of what may be described as the man-of-letters novel. It will not have escaped attention that most of these novels tend to be autobiographical. There is no reason why a writer should not put himself into his books, but there is one clear distinction between the genuine novelist and the man of letters. The novelist puts his own experiences into his book, but they are transformed in the process. A book like *Adolphe* is both autobiographical and genuine creation. The man of letters does not create; he lives partly in the actual world and partly in the world of fiction. His work is often entertaining and informative, but it does not possess the impact that we receive from true imaginative experience.

I think we must agree that both *Aimée* and *Florence* are examples of the man-of-letters novel, but they are more interesting, more intelligent and more talented than the exercises of most professional man-of-letters novelists. They are notable for their insight, their sensitiveness and the ingenuity with which personal problems are unravelled; and because Rivière was an eminent representative of the intellectual life of this time they are documents of absorbing interest.

V

The Literary Critic

I

'His critical works', wrote Mr T. S. Eliot in the memorial number of the *Nouvelle Revue Française*, 'combine a precision which is free from rigidity, with intellectual suppleness and finesse. For a mind like mine, which is too prone to measure everything by rules derived from a dogmatic conception of literature that tends more and more to become rigid and formalist, the critical method practised by Rivière is an excellent discipline.'[95]

It is an admirable description of Rivière's peculiar virtues. We are sometimes moved in England to complain that French criticism is too abstract, that French critics fasten on a single theory and use it to explain not merely the entire output of an individual writer, but a whole period or even a whole literature. The charge is not altogether without foundation. In a country where philosophy very properly forms part of the normal secondary school curriculum, men tend to think systematically. The result is that nearly all the distinguished French critics of the last century tried to create 'systems' even when they repudiated the term and claimed like Taine to be using a 'method'. A training in philosophy ought to be a help to the critic, but in France this has not always been so. It encourages the Frenchman's natural tendency to abstract speculation, is a perpetual invitation to the logical mind to build up an order in which comprehensiveness is sacrificed to external coherence. Instead of improving the standards of practical criticism, systems usually carry the critic farther and farther away from his texts, which become a mere excuse for the discussion of abstract problems only indirectly connected with them. That is why French criticism is rich in generalisations about the nature of art, but often provides little assistance in the appreciation of particular authors, and why with a critic like Taine literature is so much the handmaid of a dogmatic conception of life that it degenerates into a minor branch of sociology or history.

Rivière's training in philosophy stood him in good stead. It enabled him to appreciate to the full the implications of the work that he was discussing, but his philosophical scepticism prevented him from overlooking its literary merits because they happened to be at variance with some private system. No one had a deeper sense of the need for a clearly defined philosophy of life, but no one had a deeper distrust of the neat formula, the facile solution. It is his honesty and integrity, his sensitive response to his texts which give Rivière's criticism its balance and which relate him to Baudelaire and Bourget—a critic who has never had his due—and distinguish him from Sainte-Beuve and Taine.

2

Mr. Eliot remarks in the same note that Rivière's early work seems to him to reveal an enthusiasm which was sometimes too partial, and that the outlook displayed in his later writings was wider and more tolerant. His criticism does indeed divide neatly into two periods—the work done before and after the first war—and it is impossible not to be impressed by the way in which he matured during his four years' captivity. His earliest critical essays began to appear in periodicals in 1906-7 and are collected in *Études* and *Nouvelles études*. I do not want to underrate the charm and usefulness of this early work. It is sensitive, enthusiastic, and has moments of considerable insight, but it is essentially the work of a young man. Not only does Rivière employ the impressionist method, but there is something very personal about his approach to his authors. He is not the detached critic formulating theories and passing judgment on writers. He writes only about those authors who have a special fascination for him and with whom he feels able to enter into a personal relationship. 'He describes himself,' he wrote of Baudelaire in 1910, 'only in order to make accomplices. He gives himself to us only so that we shall give ourselves to him.'[96] It is clearly the view of a young man who is very anxious to become an 'accomplice', 'to get to know his own heart', as he puts it in the same essay, and who thinks that poetry is the means of doing so.

The personal factor is still more in evidence in the long study of Claudel written in 1906-7. He wrote it shortly after the beginning of his correspondence with Claudel and it is apparent that the exposé of Claudel's teaching is primarily an attempt to solve the critic's own religious problems. But even in these early essays his enthusiasm is infectious. In spite of the personal element his approach is concrete and his arguments are amply illustrated by quotations. We can hardly re-read the Baudelaire or the Gide today without picking up once again the *Fleurs du mal* or *La Porte étroite*. His weaknesses are most apparent when he attempts to write in a severely technical manner: 'They are not the books of a poet', he observes of Gide. 'Gide's style does not *recreate* things; it does not restore them to our eyes. We must not ask him to make the universe sensible to us.'[97] This is well said and rightly emphasises that, in spite of all the talk about the *prosateur lyrique*, the qualities of Gide's best work are those of a prose writer. We can scarcely say the same of some of the other parts of the essay: 'De là ces phrases qui commencent plusieurs fois, qui sont pleines de naissances intérieures; sitôt ouvertes, elles s'interrompent pour se reprendre, elles entrevoient une cime plus voluptueuse d'où elles reviennent s'élancer. . .'[98] It seems to me that in spite of a superficial brilliance, this sort of writing is pretending to be something that it is not, that the object is not there. Instead of seizing the movement of the prose, the emotion infiltrates slightly through the imagery—'une cime plus voluptueuse'—which is not used to illustrate the critic's thought, but to repair the defects of his analysis. The emotion is alien to the theme, and phrases like 'naissances intérieures' are no more than a superior form of verbiage.

The two most substantial pieces of criticism that Rivière wrote before the war are the essay on 'Le Roman d'Aventure' and the monograph on Rimbaud which first appeared in the *Nouvelle Revue Française* in 1913 and 1914. I propose to discuss the study of Rimbaud first because 'Le Roman d'Aventure' brings out more clearly the link between Rivière's pre-war and post-war criticism.

The Rimbaud is still the work of a young man who is seeking a message from literature, and there is a good deal of special pleading at the close. 'Rimbaud', said Rivière, 'est séparé de nous d'une manière constitutionnelle'; but it is less easy to agree when he argues that though not a Christian at the time when he wrote, he is 'un merveilleux introducteur au christianisme'.[99] In spite of this, however, it is in many ways Rivière's most sustained piece of 'practical criticism', and it remains one of the essential books on Rimbaud. The technical criticism is altogether more convincing than anything to be found in the two essays on Baudelaire and Gide; the arguments are cogent and, in a region where nearly everything is guesswork, Rivière's highly ingenious guesses are as likely to be right as anyone else's.

'Rimbaud begins by anger and abuse', but the flow of vituperation and the emphasis on *ordure* are caused by the sense of his own innocence, of being uncontaminated by the world he is denouncing: 'For we must be clear about the deep significance of these *peintures ordurières*. They are the verification by a being who is intact of terrestrial infirmity, the contemplation of sin and its consequences by one who has been preserved from them.'[100] We may feel inclined to smile when we hear that 'Rimbaud is the being who is exempt from original sin', but Rivière was surely right in suggesting that the abuse in the early poems is functional, is an attempt to demolish, symbolically, the world and its infirmities.[101] In the mature work there is, according to Rivière, an attempt to put something in its place, or rather to discover and to reach another world. This is the most original and interesting part of the essay. He draws attention to the tendency of the world described in the *Illuminations* to disintegrate and quotes the opening of 'Nocturne Vulgaire': 'Un souffle ouvre des brèches opératiques dans les cloisons,—brouille le pivotement des toits rongés,—disperse les limites des foyers,—éclipse les croisées.'

He comments:

> A hiatus forms; a sly and mysterious chink appears in things and disabuses them of the idea that they are held together. There is in Rimbaud a motif which might be called the crevice or the breach. In a corner of the picture something suddenly happens which threatens its solidity, an imperceptible fissure which climbs, goes down again and spreads, a tear which opens and extends. The damage always begins at the top of the picture.[102]

The world of external perception falls to pieces before our eyes. 'The houses no longer follow one another'; but unless there were something behind it, the result would be meaningless and chaotic:

> Rimbaud's art and *métier* imply the existence of an external object. All his methods belong to a person who is watching something, who has turned to look at something and who is describing it. His work would be incomprehensible if we did not suppose the existence of this X. It is this that gives unity to the different devices that he uses. . . Suppress it, and Rimbaud is no more than an acrobat performing a series of the

vainest and most contradictory exercises. His manner of writing collapses; he is simply doing tricks which are so ill-devised that they destroy one another. On the other hand, as soon as you restore the object mentally, everything becomes organised and falls into place.[103]

This is driven home by an effective passage of technical criticism. He compares Rimbaud's 'open' sentence with Baudelaire's 'closed' sentence:

A poem of Baudelaire's is a closed system; everything in it points towards the interior; the lines hold together like people sitting in a circle. It is because the object expressed is a feeling, is something entirely contained in the mind which surrounds and encloses it. If, on the contrary, Rimbaud's style always points outwards, it can only be because it is concentrated on something which is external to the mind.[104]

It is an extremely ingenious hypothesis, and whether or not we agree that Rimbaud discovered a new realm behind the world of common experience or that he is 'a marvellous introduction to Christianity', it does offer a possible way through the labyrinth of the *Illuminations*.

It has been said that the path of the literary critic is strewn with dead enthusiasms. This observation helps us to understand and to sympathise with the standpoint adopted by Rivière in his remarkable essay on *Le Roman d'Aventure*. He himself has spoken of the immense fascination that the Symbolist poets possessed for him when he was a schoolboy. We remember that the reading of a poem of Henri de Régnier's was the beginning of his friendship with Alain-Fournier, that the later Symbolists were among his earliest admirations and that he declared, in one of his letters to Fournier, that 'Symbolism was the true poetry because it abolished the oratorical poetry of Romanticism'.[105] Rivière's enthusiasm for the Symbolists was not as complete or as wholehearted as Fournier's—he never understood what Fournier saw in Laforgue—because he was temperamentally a classicist. We can see now, though it was not apparent at the time, that what first attracted him in Rimbaud and Claudel was not the qualities which they shared with the Symbolists but those which revealed a movement away from them. *Le Roman d'Aventure* is a transitional work. Its best pages are a brilliant but onesided criticism of the Symbolists. Rivière has escaped from the enchanted gardens and is looking at them from outside and reflecting on their apparent tawdriness. He is also groping towards the new conception of classicism which will dominate his post-war criticism.

We are living at one of those moments at which we suddenly notice that something has shifted. . . There is something which is no more, which has quietly gone out and from which every writer who wants to live must now detach himself. It is Symbolism. Like Impressionism, it has had a pretty long old age. It lingered on for years after passing its point of perfection. Yet it is dead and there is no longer anything to be done by following the path that it had opened up.[106]

He goes on to discuss what may be called the moral implications of Symbolism:

Symbolism is not, as its exponents were once naïve enough to make people think, a decadent art, a parodoxical and rotten fruit produced by an almost exhausted sap. . . But it cannot be disputed that it is an art of extreme consciousness, the art of people who are terribly aware of what they are thinking, of what they want and of what they are doing. It is not a matter of chance that it developed first and almost exclusively in this country. It could only come into being with a people whose long habit of interior examination had made them experts in self-divination and self-discovery. It could only flourish in a society of people who were very alert about themselves and quick to track down the nature and meaning of the least of their feelings. Thanks to its long psychological past, France alone provided it with a favourable soil. How could we imagine a Mallarmé who was not a Frenchman?[107]

This is Rivière's first attempt to isolate the specifically French qualities in literature. He succeeds in showing not merely that Symbolism was essentially French, but that its weaknesses, or what appeared to him to be its weaknesses, were due first to the exaggeration of characteristically French qualities, and secondly to the absence of other and no less characteristically French qualities that he admired in the classical tradition.

He goes on to give an illuminating account of the method of the Symbolist poets:

Let us begin with the subject chosen by them. It is never an event, a story or even the description of a soul, the picture of a living being. It is always an emotion—an abstract emotion, completely pure and without cause or roots, an impression detached from its origin. What the author sets out to record is his emotional reaction to an object or a spectacle which remains unknown. . . Putting himself in the place of the reader, the writer vibrates in advance at the contact with the work that he has not yet written. He shivers, he is touched like a piece of metal which straightaway strikes the note he wanted to obtain from it. With his profound awareness of the emotions, he can at once feel the particular one—however delicate it may be—among all others that his story would have aroused.[108]

44

That, Rivière thought, was why the manner in which a Symbolist work is created is so 'abnormal':

> During the time that it is being carried in the brain of its author, so far from being nourished and developed, it is reduced, subsides, becomes thinner. Delicately destructive lines cross it in all directions, analyse it, decompose it. In the same way that a fire infallibly follows the rafters of a house, consuming them right into the walls, so the author's intelligence dissolves everything in his subject which acts as structure and support. It is a work of criticism rather than of creation that it accomplishes... In his mind the work is subjected not to the confused inspiration of a naïve and ignorant genius, but to all the forces of dissolution and all the acids of thought... In the end there remains nothing but a sort of perfume, a spirit, something which is imperceptible to sight or touch and which the soul alone can distinguish and gather. In other words, the Symbolist work is a work of which more than half takes place in the mind of its author.[109]

This preparation, he concludes, is negative, a chemical rather than a physiological operation. He himself could not fail to be sensitive to its extreme subtlety, but he felt that there was something badly wrong with an art which was so completely subjective, so cut off from the world of common experience and which could arouse only a *passive* instead of an *active* admiration: 'The Symbolists knew only the pleasures of tired people. They came at the end of a century which had worked very hard; they lived in the atmosphere of the end of a day.'[110] It is time, he thinks, to have done with the art of tired people and to produce something more vigorous and more vital. We really no longer have the strength to go on listening to people talking about 'fluidity', 'continuity' and 'atmosphere'. We are exasperated by the supposed shapelessness of reality. The age of Symbolism was an age of poetry, but it seems clear that we are on the threshold of an age of the novel and the drama. Instead of describing emotions divorced from their origins, the writer must deal with something real. The new novel will be long; it will even contain *longueurs*; but it will also contain a whole world of characters who, though they may come to resemble their creator, will at the outset be absolutely distinct from him.

One of the main virtues of the new novel will be the element of unpredictability:

> In the French novel the character gradually organises himself round a theoretical core which is in a sense his definition... The statue gradually comes to life, but it has been preceded and brought into being by the Idea of itself... In a word, in the French novel the character is always the incarnation of a certain *caractère intelligible*. In the new novel, on the contrary,

the particular traits of the character will come first and will precede its essence. . . It will be an inhabited work and the proprietor will not be able to do anything except open the door for us.[111]

The Symbolists, said Rivière, lived in a state of 'memory', but the novelist will live in a state of 'adventure'. The new novel will therefore be a *roman d'aventure*. He seems to equate 'adventure' with 'action', which explains the unpredictable element:

Adventure is what happens, what is added, what comes on top of everything else, is something that we could have done without. A *roman d'aventure* is a recital of events which are not contained in one another. We never see the present emerge ready-made from the past; the progress of the work is never a deduction.[112]

The emotion that we demand from the *roman d'aventure* is the opposite of the poetic emotion. It is the sense of waiting for something, of not yet knowing everything, of being led as near as possible to the edge of what does not yet exist.[113]

He goes on to explain that he is using the term *roman d'aventure* in a personal sense. He does not mean the novels of Conan Doyle. He means a psychological *roman d'aventure* and the nearest approach that he can find to it in the past is *Wuthering Heights*, *Great Expectations* and *The Possessed*. Stendhal is somewhat surprisingly omitted from the list.

He makes another important point. The new novel will be 'classical'. He has shed the illusion that Symbolism was in some way an antidote to Romanticism. He declares roundly that Romanticism is 'an inferior form of art'[114]: 'All that we blame in it—superficial contrasts, pompous expressions, inappropriate magnificence, being grandiose at any price—can be traced to a certain lack of application.'[115]

Since the basic weakness of Romanticism was 'lack of application', it follows that the first thing we expect of the new art is careful workmanship. It must, in the words of Descartes' *Fourth Meditation*, be 'perfect and complete in all its parts'. He is careful to emphasise that this does not mean that it will be like the works of the seventeenth century, that there can be no question of going backwards, no question of a 'revival of classicism' of the kind later sponsored by Massis.

Finally, the new novel will be a monster. It will appear covered with excrescences. Interminable recitals of events will interrupt the main story, confessions, pages from a diary. the exposition of doctrines professed by one of the characters. It will form a sort of natural conglomeration, a cake of earth and stones whose elements hold together without anyone knowing

46

how. We shall lose sight of its direction, its thread. With pro-
longations on all sides it will be like those sea creatures which
move forward in any direction. We must make the best of it.
The novel that we are waiting for will not possess the lovely
rectilinear composition, the harmonious sequence and the
simplicity of narrative which have hitherto been the virtues of
the French novel.[116]

'Covered with excrescences. Interminable recitals of events
interrupting the main story, confessions, pages from a diary, the
exposition of doctrines professed by one of the characters'—it
sounds exactly like a description of the *Faux-monnayeurs*, which was
not published until 1925. Gide certainly read and admired
Rivière's essay, but there is no reason to suppose that he was influenced by it or that the passage was more than a lucky guess.[117]
It is interesting, however, to see what became of Rivière's other
prophecies. 'Le Roman d'Aventure' was published in the *Nouvelle Revue Française* in May, June and July 1913. In November
of the same year the first volumes of *A la Recherche du temps perdu*
appeared, and the following year Joyce began to write *Ulysses*.
They are, perhaps, the only other two European novels which
conformed in any fundamental way to Rivière's definition. They
are both very long and they both undoubtedly have *longueurs*;
and they have both been described at different times as 'classical'. What is interesting is the nature of their classicism. Rivière
proceeded on the assumption that Symbolism was 'dead' and
that the 'new novel' would reveal a complete break with the
immediate past. Now this certainly did not happen. It did not
happen because the development of literature is not, as it might
appear to a young man writing immediately before the outbreak
of the first World War, a series of sharp changes of direction, the
death of one movement and the birth of a fresh one. It is a process of continual slight alteration or, to put it in another way,
literature implies an internal critical activity, a constant revision
of what seems dead in the immediate past and the exploitation of
qualities which are latent in it because certain qualities are perennial and are native to all good writing. This is what occurred
in the nineteenth century. The Romantics revolted against the
degenerate classicism of the eighteenth century and tried to
bring back life, colour and imagery into poetry. The reaction
naturally went too far. There is a good deal of justice in Rivière's
criticism of Romanticism, but like his criticism of Symbolism it
is too youthfully sweeping. Baudelaire, writing in the Romantic
aftermath, put matters a little differently. He spoke of the need
of 'a prosody whose roots thrust deeper into the human soul
than is indicated by any classical theory', and of 'the possibility
of expressing every sensation of sweetness or bitterness, beatitude
or horror, by linking a particular substantive with a particular
adjective which was analogous or contrary to it'. He wrote:

Certainly it would be an injustice to deny the services rendered by the school known as Romantic. It recalled us to the truth of the image; it destroyed the academic commonplaces, and even from the superior point of view of linguistics, it does not deserve the contempt with which it has been iniquitously covered by certain impotent pedants. But by its very principle, the Romantic rebellion was condemned to shortsightedness. . . In the name of the higher principles which constitute universal life, we have the right to declare it guilty of heterodoxy.[118]

Baudelaire himself has been well described as a 'counter-Romantic'. We find in his work many of the weaknesses of Romanticism, but we also find the strength which came from combining what was sound in it with the perennial qualities of poetry. History repeated itself at the time of Symbolism. The early work of Laforgue, Rimbaud and Mallarmé contains imitations of Baudelaire, but in their mature work they rejected what seemed to them to be no longer vital in Baudelaire and went on to discover fresh forms. Rivière's essay is an exceptionally acute criticism of the weaknesses of Symbolism, but he mistook the part for the whole. He failed to see that Symbolism had brought something new into poetry which was of permanent value and that it could not simply be written off as 'dead'. The subsequent history not merely of French, but of European poetry has shown that Symbolism is still a living force and that poetry can never be the same as it was before the Symbolists.

This is what happened with the *roman d'aventure*. Mr Eliot has described the 'classical' elements in *Ulysses*, and as Rivière was to show in some of the finest of his post-war criticism, combined a startling originality with qualities which belonged pre-eminently to the French classical tradition. It is also true, however, that both novelists retained a great deal of what was best in Symbolism and that without its example they would certainly not have achieved all they did. That is why the perfect definition of Proust's style seems to me to be Crémieux's *classicisme impressionniste*.

3

When we turn to Rivière's post-war criticism, we find that it is very largely a development of the position that he adopted in *Le Roman d'Aventure*. His standpoint in that essay is highly individual, but it is already much less personal than anything that he had written previously. One of the first things that strikes us about his later work is that there is no attempt to extract a private 'message' from his authors. In the manifesto that he wrote for the *Nouvelle Revue Française* when it resumed publication in June 1919, he told his readers that the aim of its founders had been to provide a place which was propitious to creative work and to ensure that it was well stocked by means of an intelligent criticism.

Rather than evolve slogans and prescribe rules, they applied themselves to clearing away undergrowth of every sort. I mean by that preoccupations of a utilitarian, theoretical or moral nature which might hinder or deform the spontaneous vegetation of genius or talent.[119]

Today, like yesterday, and in spite of millions of dead, it remains true that a work of art is beautiful for reasons which are absolutely intrinsic and which can only be unravelled by direct study and by a sort of *corps à corps* with the work itself.[120]

One of the greatest evils of the war had been to absorb men's minds. 'It had begun to dictate all their thoughts. They could no longer find anything by themselves. They even ceased to be able to look at an object in front of them. They could not see what it was, but only what it ought to be.'[121]

The aim of the review was to help people to rid themselves of the constraint that the war still exercised over them. This could only be done by criticism, 'by discerning, choosing and recommending'. At this point Rivière returns to the attack on Symbolism:

We shall show that Symbolism and all its derivatives are simply the means, which in future will be powerless, of multiplying *in extremis* Romanticism's chances of survival and providing it for a time with a sort of artificial respiration.

Put more simply, we shall try to reveal what is out-of-date in the cultivation of the means of expression for their own sake and independently of the value of what is expressed, in the purely musical researches in poetry, in the lyrical presentation of facts, in the direct recording of states of sensibility, in what may be called the global manner of explaining psychological reality.[122]

Finally:

We salute the claims of the intelligence which today is clearly seeking to recover its rights in art; not in order to supplant sensibility completely, but in order to penetrate, analyse and rule over it.[123]

The most important parts of the manifesto are the assertion that 'a work of art is beautiful for reasons which are absolutely intrinsic' and the determination to get rid of any sort of utilitarian, moral or theoretical preoccupations. This view was stated in still more radical fashion in the essay called 'La Crise du Concept de Littérature', which was published in 1924 and is a complete condemnation of 'messages':

49

If, in the seventeenth century, anyone had taken it into his head to ask Molière or Racine why they wrote, they would probably only have been able to answer: 'To amuse decent people'. It was only with Romanticism that the act of writing began to be thought of as a raid on the absolute and its result as a revelation. At this time literature garnered the heritage of religion and organised itself on the model of the thing it was replacing. The writer became a priest; the sole aim of his gestures was to produce in the host that literature had become 'the real presence'. The whole of nineteenth-century literature is a vast incantation towards the miraculous.[124]

It must be remembered that a good deal of Rivière's best work was written in the course of controversies over the main literary problems of the day and this led him to state his case in an extreme form. With this reservation, the manifesto and the essay on 'La Crise du Concept de Littérature' are an admirable presentation of the classic attitude in literature. It is rooted in the belief that all human activities are good, but it refuses to admit that one activity can ever be a substitute for another. Any attempt to make it so leads to a confusion which is highly detrimental to literature. One of the most important functions of criticism was to prevent this confusion, to clear away 'undergrowth' and to ensure that literature did not degenerate into a vapid religiosity or engage in the sterile exploration of technique for its own sake.

Rivière's classicism was not a system; it had nothing in common with Brunetière's. It was based on a deeply felt awareness of the continuity of the French tradition, and one of his most interesting and provocative feats was to establish a direct connection between Racine and Proust. The whole of his later criticism is rooted in his sense of the great classic writers as a living force and this made his criticism of Romanticism, which had once been too sweeping, lucid and deadly. What he admired in Racine was that master's power of translating his perceptions directly into words without allowing his immediate experience to be distorted by preconceived ideas; and what he disliked in Rousseau, whose literary ability he fully admitted, was the way in which the *données* were modified and distorted until literature became a substitute for religion or a branch of moral philosophy.

One of his most original pieces of criticism is his study of Racine. The short lecture on *Andromaque* in *Moralisme et littérature* does more than any other modern work to demolish the 'tender' Racine of the nineteenth-century myth and to restore the true Racine whose ferocity shocked his own age as it delights ours. The distinguished critics of the last century were inclined to insist too much on Racine's elegance and to overlook the destructive force of passion in his plays and the extraordinary insight into human emotions which Sainte-Beuve referred to somewhat vaguely in the *Portraits littéraires* as his 'savante métaphysique du coeur'. Rivière said of a character in *Andromaque*:

There is therefore nothing in his mind which so to speak acts as a dyke against the wave of love except a contrary wave which he calls anger, resentment, hate or what you will, but which at bottom is of the same nature and the same stuff as the passion against which it is pitted and which in the last resort is no more than the flow of the same passion turned against itself.[125]

In a comment on the line: 'Leur haine ne fera qu'irriter sa tendresse' he remarks:

This is the basic principle and even the postulate of Racine's psychology, which is formulated with an absolute clarity. He displays what I feel inclined to call the pure or direct contact between feelings and their way of modifying one another instantaneously. There is no intervention of reason or reflection. . . No [Pylade]foresees, knows that their hatred will act as a direct irritant on Pyrrhus' *tendresse* for Andromaque. Nothing can prevent the friction. There is, if one can use the expression, an absence of any sheath in the feelings as Racine describes them and this makes them perpetually naked for one another. . .

When, a moment or two ago, I used the word *dissolu*, I gave it, mentally, its full meaning including its etymological meaning. I meant that feelings are described by Racine without there being anything that attaches them; the core of the mind in which they are perceived seems to have crumbled away. Everything that could act as a cement between them, everything that *composes* them, has been suppressed.[126]

We must go further than this [he writes a page or two later]. We must show at work in Racine's characters those ferments of dissolution, those forces which destroy the personality, that modern French writers are blamed for analysing too complacently in their work. Almost all Racine's characters, or at any rate those in whom the poet manages to interest us, are characters who fall to pieces (*des personnages qui se défont*).[127]

I claim that Racine's indifference to morality enabled him, and alone could enable him, to seize the workings of the mind in their darkest but their most real spontaneity. His way of putting aside what is factitious and noting what is immediate in the human heart is properly speaking miraculous.[128]

This is not a plea for a shallow amoralism in literature. Rivière believed that the claim of truth was paramount, and in his study of Racine he anticipates the theory of the *sainteté de la vérité* which has since become familiar in the work of writers like Maritain. It must be remembered that the lecture on Racine was part of a public debate with Ramon Fernandez and it is possible that his thesis carried him too far in the last passage.[129] He seems to me to confuse the moral attitude of Racine's *characters* with the attitude of the *author* towards them. There was undoubtedly an element of complicity in Racine's representation of the moral collapse of his characters, but it is going too far to assume that he necessarily approved of the moral tone of the world he created. Rivière's contention that he did not interfere with his characters by introducing irrelevant moral considerations is, however, perfectly sound and this distinction made possible his searching criticism of Rousseau and the Romantic novel in the same lectures:

In other words, Rousseau does not tell us about his loves and hates, his pleasures and his *ennuis*, but about his magnanimity and his baseness. 'I have shown myself as I am; contemptible and vile when I was, good, generous, sublime when I was.' In this way he initiates, inaugurates a certain manner of perceiving feelings only when they are qualified, of perceiving the qualifications instead of the feelings, which seems to me to be most dangerous.

Dangerous in what sense?—In this: when he uses the words contemptible or generous, sincere or lying, you no longer have any precise impression. The specific qualities of the feeling, its form, its movement, which we were admiring a few minutes ago when rendered by Racine, disappear. There is something vague and infinite which is introduced into the mind by means of the judgments, whatever they happen to be, that are passed on it.

I do not mean to say that Rousseau does not succeed in giving us any idea of his personality. On the contrary, we see it in marvellous relief, but there remains about it something matt, opaque, 'overcast' in the sense in which we use the word to describe the weather.[130]

Rivière considered that Rousseau was to blame for most of the excesses of the Romantic novel. 'We find', he said, 'that the whole of Romantic fiction is spoilt by a certain moral preconception'. Of their characters he asked:

Where do these beings come from? They are born of a certain moral image: purity, greatness, innocence, sublime nobility or, on the contrary, infamy, bottomless perfidy, unspeakable baseness, unadulterated perversity, or again sadness, disgust with life, magnificent disdain, gloomy disinterestedness. That is what their authors have in front of them before they have even begun to outline their characters. That is the scheme from which they are extracted.[131]

What I mean is this. The Romantic habit of imagining the [moral] qualities of a character before the character himself, or rather of extracting the character from certain pure and abstract qualities, takes us outside psychology and leads to absolute poetry. Put still more generally, Rousseau leads to

Rimbaud. As soon as values are introduced into psychology, you get monsters; and as soon as you get monsters, you are out of touch with life.[132]

According to Rivière, art springs from a conflict between the individual and the world in which he is living.[133] The art can only be genuine provided that it remains in contact with the real world, provided that the individual and his milieu are real and not simply 'monsters' battling in a world of phantasy. This meant that the artist was bound to accept the world as given in common experience: 'All the classics were implicitly positivists. They accepted the fact of an internal and an external world and the obligation to get to know it. Its degree of reality or whether it happened to be a mere fulguration of their own ego mattered little to them. They accepted its limit in all simplicity.'[134]

The existence of a clearly defined outer world has a normative influence on the artist's experience, but Rivière was careful to emphasise that the artist must begin with a knowledge of himself:

There can be no really profound description of characters which is not based on a close and solid knowledge of oneself. Before turning outwards with any chance of success, analysis must have delved deeply inside. . . What was lacking in Flaubert and the novelists of his school was that they had not begun by understanding themselves. Because they wanted to be directly objective from the start, they were condemned to plant mere *objects* in front of themselves without animating them, without giving them any variety and without illuminating them from within.

Proust sees everything, even external things, from the same angle that he sees himself. . . In this way he rejoins the great classic tradition. Does Racine ever do anything except seek other people in himself?. . . There is, properly speaking, nothing here that can be called *creation*, but simply invention, that is to say, something is *found*, perceived, unravelled; a detection, if we can put it in this way, of the consciousness of others.[135]

He uses the words 'creation' and 'invention' in a rather personal sense. 'Creation' had for him certain romantic associations. It suggested 'monsters', 'absolute poetry', 'loss of contact with life'. 'Invention', on the other hand, meant the exploration of a given world, but it did not in any sense exclude the discovery of new combinations of feelings as we can see from his study of Racine.

M. Jean Schlumberger has said that Proust intoxicated Rivière 'with the idea that the genius of the French consisted uniquely in the penetration of its analysis'.[136] He certainly set great store by it, but this criticism seems to me to do him an injustice. He was very conscious of the limitations of the French approach and his criticism of them in a brilliant essay called 'De Dostoïewsky et de l'Insondable' displays the same flexibility and breadth of outlook as his criticism of the French mind in *Le Français*. Once a novelist has the idea of a character in his mind, he says, there are two very different ways of working it out. He can either insist on its 'complexity' or he can emphasise its 'coherence'. He will either want to *produce* it in all its 'obscurity' or he will suppress the obscurity for the benefit of the reader. He will either seal off or he will explore the dark places of the soul. Dostoievsky naturally chose the way of exploration; most of the French novelists chose 'coherence'. Rivière, as we have seen, had already drawn attention to the tendency of French novelists to 'organise their characters round a theoretical core', and he proceeds to develop this view in the essay on Dostoievsky:

When faced with the complexity of the human soul and as we seek to represent it, we also seek instinctively to organise it. Our very description is an attempt at integration. Something in us, that we are unable to master, at once comes into play and shows us the internal fastenings of the model, the solidarity of its different aspects. If need be, we give it the finishing touch. We suppress a few small divergent traits; we interpret a few obscure details in the manner most favourable to the construction of a psychological unity.

When we draw the portrait of a character, it is repugnant to us to leave anything indefinite in it. 'Il y avait du je ne sais quoi dans tout Monsieur de la Rochefoucauld', writes the Cardinal de Retz. That is precisely it. He expresses it so that the reader shall not be left to sense it for himself.

We never leave any gaps in the character whom we have brought into being through which unforeseen inspirations could reach him. When we make him speak, there are no inexplicable overtones and nothing is ever heard which sounds a different note for the mind and for the imagination. We penetrate into all the chinks of his character with our busy wax and we cement them. A complete sealing off of its abysses—that is the ideal towards which we tend. And I imagine that it is this which must embarrass foreigners in Racine's Néron or even in Stendhal's Julien. We never express the giddiness of the human soul.

We may very well conceive that rather than to send the mind straying towards a psychological infinite, the task of the novelist is to bring it back to an event which is mysterious, but concrete and measurable.[137]

'Dostoievsky', he adds, 'was the first writer who made me aware of our insufficiency on this point'. He goes on to say that the French must be on their guard against their tendency to simplify, to reduce everything to a common denominator, but that provided that they never let it take precedence over the complexity of human nature, it will enable them to show links which are real and form part of man's psychic nature.

In the essay on 'Marcel Proust et la Tradition Classique', published in 1920, Rivière had suggested some of the ways in which Proust 'rejoined the great classic tradition'. In another essay on 'Proust et l'Esprit Positif', which appeared in 1923 a year after the Dostoievsky, he tries to show that Proust and the French classics were free from the particular 'insufficiency' that he detected in the contemporary French novel. Proust like Freud was aware that one of the principal functions of our feelings is to lie to us. It is therefore the duty of the psychologist and the writer to resist the evidence that feelings give about themselves and the form in which they try to present themselves to us. The discovery that 'distrust is the mother of penetration' is not altogether a modern one. The great classics from Montaigne to La Rochefoucauld and La Bruyère, from Racine to Marivaux and Laclos, would never have managed to give us that sensation of truth, which we do not find to the same degree in any other literature, if they had not begun by adopting a radically sceptical attitude towards themselves and 'the insinuations of their hearts'. Although Proust shared their scepticism, his critical attitude towards feelings and his determined rejection of the conventional categories of experience went much further.

Proust's work on human feeling is of a kind that is absolutely new. Whether it was admitted or not, up to the present when studying feelings writers started out from a conception of consciousness to which they were bound to return at the end of the book. I do not say that Proust did not have a law to guide him as well, or rather that he did not erect into a principle, a postulate, his doubt about existence itself and about the unity of consciousness... *The essential thing is that he repudiated all psychological entities and set out from pure experience.* Of course he moved towards a law and formulated it as soon as he saw it emerging; but he was ready to abandon it and forget it as soon as he saw another law emerge which contradicted it.[138]

M. Schlumberger has suggested that Rivière's immense enthusiasm for Proust was a 'phase' that he would have outgrown as he outgrew his enthusiasm for Gide and Claudel when they had served his purpose.[139] Few critics escape the charge of sometimes putting into their authors what they want to find in them. I have never been able to see in Meredith the things that Rivière found in him, but he does seem to me to make good his case in his essays on Proust.

When we compare the different texts which have been quoted here, we can see that Rivière moved steadily forward from the early formulations in *Le Roman d'Aventure* to an entirely new conception of classicism. It is not a system or a doctrine or even strictly speaking a theory. His classicism is something that is essentially organic, something that is constantly growing and developing. It is not a matter of rules, but an attitude of mind. I think that we might conclude that is something which is very close to what Mr Eliot calls 'the mind of Europe'.

We have seen the danger of the French tendency 'to simplify, to reduce everything to a common denominator', but it is by no means the only danger that faces the contemporary writer. It will be generally agreed that literature has been profoundly altered by the discredit into which the classical metaphysic has fallen, and the rise of the idealist philosophies. The result of this change, said Rivière, was the writer's progressive loss of faith in the reality of the external world and a retreat into the world within. This meant the end of the conflict between the man and his milieu, which for Rivière was the starting point of nearly all good art, and the predominance of pure 'creation': 'The writer feels his creative power taking precedence over his perception. . . Creation, immediate and continuous creation, becomes his only help and his only duty.'[140] Rivière studies the effect of this change on nineteenth-century literature and language in some detail in the two essays called 'Reconnaissance à Dada' and 'Marcel Proust et la Tradition Classique'. I have not room for more than two quotations, but they illustrate the extraordinary intuition, the faculty for going straight to the root of the matter, which is one of his greatest gifts:

> From Stendhal onwards, there sets in a continuous degradation of our ancient, inveterate faculty of understanding and rendering feeling. Flaubert represents the moment at which the evil becomes sensible and alarming. I do not mean that *Madame Bovary* and *L'Éducation sentimentale* show no knowledge of the human heart; but neither of them reveals the slightest sign of a direct view into its complexity; neither carries us a step forward in our knowledge of it or gives us a frontal view of fresh aspects of it. There is in the writer a certain heaviness of intelligence in relation to his sensibility; it follows his sensibility badly; it no longer unravels it; it can no longer penetrate into its caprices or its nuances.[141]

This should be set beside his criticism of Mallarmé's use of language:

> It was with Mallarmé and with Rimbaud (we might go even farther back as Flaubert is not without responsibility in this respect) that words first showed signs of being debauched. I naturally regard as very brilliant and very important the discovery of that mysterious virtue in them which is distinct from their virtue of signification and which allows them to absorb a little of the writer's sensibility and to carry it, in the form of a simple seed, into another world where it will bloom again. No one admires more than I the way in which with

Mallarmé words detach themselves very gently from their individual meaning, then from their logical solidarity simply in order to finish... But on this interpretation they cease to be signs and assume a value which is post-intellectual. In future their appearance will be determined solely by their internal relationship with the subject [he means the writer]... The danger is immense. For since the resemblance of one or other of them with the subject can be appreciated only by the subject, nothing prevents it from being recognised in every case. Every word, from the moment it is produced or simply envisaged by thought in a flash, has a relation with it. Since it has come into the writer's thoughts, every word expresses them because nothing can have put it there except precisely its aptitude to express them, whether they are comprehensible or not. Every word therefore is justifiable, is expressive, arriving after any other word, presented in any connection and revealing anything you like.[142]

This is an extreme statement of the case against Flaubert and Mallarmé; but though the criticism may appear severe it was surely a correct diagnosis of the tendencies at work in those writers. The aim of the essay was to show that Romanticism led logically to Surrealism, that the work of Flaubert, Mallarmé and even Rimbaud represented stages in the same process. It gives precision to the criticisms of Symbolism originally made in *Le Roman d'Aventure*, and when we look at the later essay as a whole, it seems to me that Rivière proves his case up to the hilt.

In his mature work Rivière asserts once again that we cannot put the clock back. 'We must take advantage', he writes, 'of the great operation carried out by Rousseau and Romanticism, that is to say, the introduction of the individual into literature'.[143] But we must also 'renounce subjectivism, effusion, pure creation, the transmigration of the ego and the disregard of the object which have plunged us into the void... The mind must recover its faith in a reality which is distinct from its creative power and come to distinguish in itself again an instrument and a substance.'[143]

I think that it can now be seen that Rivière was strong where so many distinguished French critics have been painfully weak. He possessed a perfectly clear conception of the function of literature; he wrote his criticism from a definite standpoint; but instead of allowing this to distort his sensibility and narrow the scope of his work, he turned it into a source of strength. It gives his work a breadth and clarity which are rare in French criticism. He did not try to fit literature into some personal philosophical system; he saw clearly the lines along which it was developing; and he used criticism not to demolish theories for purely polemical purposes, but to try to influence the artist. Few modern critics, indeed, have possessed a more realistic conception of 'the function of criticism at the present time'.

57

Conclusion

I said at the beginning of this essay that Rivière was one of the most characteristic representatives of contemporary French intellectual life. I also said that the vicissitudes of the age were reflected in his writings. I was not thinking purely of the professional *tourmenté* that he undoubtedly was. When we look at his life and writings as a whole, we are aware of their consistency, of a pattern which runs through all of them. One of the first things that strikes us is the existence of an obstacle and Rivière's opposition to it. 'Our friendship', he said of his meeting with Fournier, 'was not immediate. We became aware of our differences of character before our resemblances.' 'I needed at any price', says the hero of *Aimée*, 'some one different, some one alien to me, who would provide my heart with an obstacle'. We can see from his correspondence that he defined his own views in opposition first to Fournier, then to Claudel. When we look more closely, we find that like the hero of his novel Rivière was constantly trying to find a middle way between two extremes—extremes represented by Claudel and Gide in religion, France and Germany in politics, classicism and romanticism in literature.

There are certain reservations to be made. A writer's work must be seen as a whole, but though Rivière's books undoubtedly illuminate one another, we are conscious of a curious rift in the man. His literary and political criticism is extraordinarily acute, but we sometimes have the impression that we are in contact with a disembodied mind, that the man is to be found only in the correspondence, the religious writings and the novels which provide an overflow for feelings that were rigorously excluded from the criticism. This division explains a certain lack of force. His was not one of those minds which impose themselves. His virtues were sensitiveness, insight, clarity, not strength. His successes, which were sometimes precarious, were largely due to his ability to extract and combine what was best in two apparently irreconcilable attitudes. That is the secret of his particular achievement, but it explains why in the last resort he was a very distinguished writer instead of a great one.

APPENDICES

NOTES

1. Adrien Jans: *La Pensée de Jacques Rivière*, Brussels, 1938, p. 71.
2. *Miracles*, Paris, 1924, p. 13.
3. *Ibid.*, p. 18.
4. *Ibid.*, pp. 18-9.
5. *Correspondance*, new and revised edition, Paris, 1947, I, p. 238.
6. *Ibid.*, p. 296.
7. *Ibid.*, p. 312.
8. *Ibid.*, p. 300.
9. *Ibid.*, p. 185.
10. *Ibid.*, p. 135.
11. *Ibid.*, II, p. 150.
12. *Ibid.*, II, p. 245.
13. *Ibid.*, II, p. 397.
14. *Ibid.*, II, p. 63.
15. *Ibid.*, II, p. 110.
16. *Ibid.*, II, p. 159.
17. See E. J. H. Greene, 'Jules Laforgue et T. S. Eliot' in *Revue de Littérature Comparée*, 22ième année, Juillet-Septembre, 1948, p. 363.
18. T. E. Hulme, *Speculations*, London, 1924, p. 117.
19. *Correspondance*, II, pp. 254-5.
20. *Études*, Paris, 1912, p. 119.
    'He has confined himself to establishing a point of view which I find new and interesting, though it remains that of an amateur and a tourist.' (Claudel's comment on the essay in a letter to Gide in P. Claudel & A. Gide: *Correspondance 1899-1926*, Paris, 1949, p. 207.)
21. J. Rivière & P. Claudel: *Correspondance*, Paris, 1926, pp. 2, 5-6.
22. *Ibid.*, p. 10.
23. *Ibid.*, pp. 37-8.
24. *Ibid.*, p. 27.
25. *Ibid.*, p. 80.
26. *Ibid.*, p. 91.
27. *Ibid.*, p. 118.
28. *Ibid.*, pp. 170-1.
29. See P. Claudel & A. Gide: *Correspondance 1899-1926*, p. 242 and Gide's *Journal* 1889-1939, Paris, 1939, pp. 359, 805.
30. J. Rivière & P. Claudel, *Correspondance*, pp. 193-4.
31. *Ibid.*, p. 197.
32. *Correspondance*, II, pp. 286-7.
33. *De la Foi*, Paris, 1927, pp. 34-5.
34. *Ibid.*, pp. 97-8.
35. *Ibid.*, pp. 101-2.
36. *A la Trace de Dieu*, Paris, 1925, p. 28.
37. *Ibid.*, p. 12.
38. *Ibid.*, p. 191.
39. *Ibid.*, pp. 173-4.
40. *De la Foi*, p. 38.
41. *A la Trace de Dieu*, p. 29.
42. *Ibid.*, p. 31.
43. *Ibid.*, p. 29.
44. *De la Foi*, p. 41.
45. *Ibid.*, pp. 48-9.
46. *Ibid.*, pp. 49-50.

47. *A la Trace de Dieu*, p. 38.

48. *Ibid.*, p. 46.

49. *Ibid.*, pp. 75-6.

50. *De la Foi*, pp. 80-1.

51. *La Nouvelle Revue Française*, No. 139, April, 1925, pp. 773, 774, 775. (Letter of 4 January 1913.)

52. *Correspondance*, II, p. 322.

53. A volume of *Études politiques* was announced for future publication in the memorial number of the *Nouvelle Revue Française* in 1925.

54. The book was first published in 1918. My references are to the eleventh edition, 1936, pp. 26-7.

55. *Ibid.*, p. 53.

56. *Ibid.*, pp. 45, 46.

57. See the chapter on 'The Loyal Population' in S. Haffner, *Germany: Jekyll and Hyde*, London, 1940.

58. *L'Allemand*, p. 60.

59. *Ibid.*, p. 71.

60. *Ibid.*, pp. 87, 88.

61. *Ibid.*, p. 72.

62. *Ibid.*, p. 103.

63. Paris, 1928. This edition was limited to 800 copies, and as it has never been reprinted, it is very difficult to obtain.

64. *Le Français*, pp. 26-7.

65. *Ibid.*, pp. 28, 40.

66. *Ibid.*, p. 33.

67. *Ibid.*, pp. 30, 31.

68. *Ibid.*, p. 49.

69. *Ibid.*, pp. 55-7.

70. *Ibid.*, pp. 102-3.

71. *Nouvelle Revue Française*, No. 92, May, 1921, p. 559.

72. *Ibid.*, p. 569.

73. *Ibid.*, p. 563.

74. *Ibid.*, p. 564.

75. *Ibid.*, pp. 564-5.

76. *Nouvelle Revue Française*, No. 106, July, 1922, p. 5.

77. *Ibid.*, pp. 8, 9.

78. *Nouvelle Revue Française*, No. 116, May, 1923, pp. 726-7.

79. *Ibid.*, p. 727.

80. *Ibid.*, pp. 728-9.

81. It was written while he was a prisoner-of-war and is said to be 'a barely disguised account' of an unhappy love affair which occurred just before the war. (Pierre Charlot: *Jacques Rivière*, Paris n.d. [1934], p. 176.)

82. 'Magnificence and gallantry have never appeared in France with so much brilliance as in the last years of Henry II's reign. The prince was gallant, well-favoured and amorous: although his passion for Diane de Poitiers, Duchesse de Valentinois, had begun twenty years earlier it was no less violent and he gave no less striking evidence of its hold over him. . .'
'When I was a child women were already an object of adoration for me. Even before I was capable of desiring them, their looks, their movement and the tender lines of their bodies produced in me an ill-defined and delicious agitation in which I submerged myself completely and passionately.'

83. 'I did not feel myself precipitated towards them. On the contrary, they appeared to me as though they were sacred, forbidden beings. I should have trembled to approach them. The emotions roused in me at the sight of them were so violent, so diverse, so tumultuous that they destroyed one another and left me where I was.'

84. Reprinted in *Nouvelles études*, Paris, 1947, pp. 220-2.

85. 'I cannot insist enough on Marthe's restfulness, on the way in which she fortified me, corrected my faults. In the same way that you restrain the rush of a torrent, I thought for a time that she would succeed in making my sensibility normal, in drawing together its *élans*, its hopes, its demands.

But I was not sufficiently balanced, sufficiently normal for such contentment to remain mine in its perfection. Although free from all vice, I was nevertheless afflicted with a perversity of a psychological order which made my contentment fatally precarious.

How am I to define this perversity?—I did not care for happiness.

Is it really that? It would be better to say that I was fond of my heart, fond of all the new ways of feeling that it invented. I believed too much in it; I awaited with too much curiosity its changes and wished too deeply that it would change.'

86. 'Her eyes. It was by her eyes that I always recognised her; they spoke to me in silence of the perversion that united us.'

87. 'I was conscious of it inside me in advance like an immense weakness, like the virtual collapse of my whole personality.'

88. 'It seemed as though I were at last on the verge of that blessed catastrophe of which I had so long dreamed.'

89. 'A certain element of badness in the depths of me which desired only to be intrigued, thrown out, reduced to despair. . . I needed at any price some one different, alien to me, who would provide my heart with an obstacle; I needed some one who wouldn't listen to me, who wouldn't give in to me.'

90. 'I had not yet taught her anything [about herself]; I allowed her delicious ignorance of the secret symmetry of our souls to be as prolonged as possible; I wanted for a time to be alone in my knowledge. . .'

'I plunged into her soul and I saw in it what I knew to be in my own: the frantic delight in feeling and its modulations, the constant need to be somebody different, the abandonment without reserve or repentance to the hand which in secret is always creating new dispositions in our hearts.'

91. 'There is only one thing in the world which matters to me: the perfection of my feelings.'

92. *Journal 1889-1939*, second edition, Paris, 1948, p. 746. (Compare: 'J'étais venu sur Aimée comme une vague trop caressante.')

93. It was also the year in which Mme Rivière published her own autobiographical novel, *Le Bouquet de roses rouges*, in which she describes the first years of her married life.

94. It is certainly difficult to reconcile it with her use of quotations from the novel —still unpublished—in her Introduction to the correspondence with Claudel.

95. *Nouvelle Revue Française*, No. 139, April, 1925, p. 658.

96. *Études*, p. 31.

97. *Ibid.*, p. 180.

98. *Ibid.*, p. 186.

99. *Rimbaud*, Paris, 1930, pp. 49, 232.

100. *Ibid.*, p. 60.

101. *Ibid.*, p. 44.

102. *Ibid.*, pp. 131-2.

103. *Ibid.*, p. 177.

104. *Ibid.*, p. 186.

105. *Correspondance*, I, p. 137.

106. *Nouvelles études*, Paris, 1947, p. 235.

107. *Ibid.*, p. 236.

108. *Ibid.*, p. 237.

109. *Ibid.*, p. 238.

110. *Ibid.*, p. 246.

111. *Ibid.*, pp. 271-2.

112. *Ibid.*, p. 273.

113. *Ibid.*, p. 277.

114. *Ibid.*, p. 251.
115. *Ibid.*, p. 253.
116. *Ibid.*, p. 268.
117. See *Journal 1889-1939*, p. 391.
118. *L'Art romantique* (Conard Edition), p. 177.
119. *Nouvelles études*, pp. 284-5.
120. *Ibid.*, p. 285.
121. *Ibid.*, p. 286.
122. *Ibid.*, pp. 289-90.
123. *Ibid.*, p. 290.
124. *Ibid.*, p. 313. Compare:
    'More and more mankind will discover that we have to turn to poetry to inter-
    pret life for us, to console us, to sustain us. Without poetry our science will appear
    incomplete; and most of what now passes for religion and philosophy will be re-
    placed by poetry' (Matthew Arnold: 'The Study of Poetry' in *Essays in Criticism*,
    Second Series).
125. *Moralisme et littérature*, Paris, 1932, p. 28.
126. *Ibid.*, pp. 31-2.
127. *Ibid.*, pp. 35-6.
128. *Ibid.*, p. 38.
129. He seems to admit this in his summing-up in the final lecture. See pp. 186 *et seq.*
130. *Ibid.*, pp. 50-1.
131. *Ibid.*, p. 68.
132. *Ibid.*, pp. 77-8.
133. *Ibid.*, pp. 188-9.
134. *Nouvelles études*, p. 300.
135. *Ibid.*, pp. 153-4.
136. *Eveils*, Paris, 1950, p. 223.
137. *Nouvelles études*, pp. 177-8, 179.
138. *Ibid.*, pp. 204-5 (Italics mine).
139. *Op. cit.*, p. 222.
140. *Nouvelles études*, p. 301.
141. *Ibid.*, pp. 151-2.
142. *Ibid.*, pp. 308-9.
143. *Moralisme et littérature*, p. 82.

BIOGRAPHICAL NOTE

1886	Jacques Rivière born at Bordeaux on 15th July.
1903	Meets Henri Alain Fournier at Lycée Lakanal, Paris.
1907	Passes *Licence ès Lettres* at Bordeaux during his military service.
1909	Marries Isabelle Fournier on 24th August.
1909-1911	Teaches at the École Saint-Joseph des Tuileries and the Collège Stanislas. Passes *diplôme d'études superieures* at the Sorbonne with a thesis on the *Théodicée de Fénelon*.
1911	Becomes secretary of the *Nouvelle Revue Française*.
1914	Called up on the outbreak of war as sergeant in the 220th Infantry. Taken prisoner at battle of Eton on the 24th August.
1914-1917	Prisoner of war at Koenigsbrück (Saxony) and reprisals camp of Hülsberg (Hanover).
1917-1918	Interned in Switzerland.
1918	Repatriated.
1919	Editor of the *Nouvelle Revue Française*.
1925	Dies on the 14th February.

PUBLISHED WORKS

(Place of publication Paris unless otherwise stated)

Études Gallimard, 1912.

L'Allemand, Gallimard, 1918.

Aimée, Gallimard, 1922.

Marcel Proust, Monaco, Société des Conférences, 1924.
> (Reproduced in *N.R.F.* for April, 1925, pp. 786-819, and in *Quelques progrès dans l'étude du coeur humain* (q.v.)

De la Foi précédé de *De la Sincérité envers soi-même*, Les Cahiers de Paris, 1ère série, Cahier VI, 1925.
> Nouvelle édition, Aux Horizons de France, 1927.

Quelques progrès dans l'étude du coeur humain Proust et Freud, Librairie de France, 1926.

A la Trace de Dieu, Gallimard, 1925.

Correspondance, 1907-1914 (J. Rivière et P. Claudel), Plon, 1926.

Correspondance, 1905-1914 (J. Rivière et Alain-Fournier), 4 vols, Gallimard, 1926-1928.
> Nouvelle édition revue et augmentée, 2 vols. 1947.

Correspondance (J. Rivière et Antonin Artaud), Gallimard, 1927.

Le Français, Claude Aveline, 1928.

Carnet de guerre, (Collection: Le Livre Neuf), Éditions de la Belle Page, 1929.

Rimbaud, Kra, 1930.
> Nouvelle édition, 1938.

Pour et contre une Société des Nations (1917-1918), Cahiers de la Quinzaine, 14ème cahier de la 19ème série, Artisan du Livre, 1930.

Moralisme et littérature (with Ramon Fernandez), Corrêa, 1932.

Florence, Corrêa, 1935.

Nouvelles etudes, Gallimard, 1947.

ENGLISH TRANSLATIONS

Letters to a Doubter, London: Burns, Oates & Washbourne, 1930 (Translation of Correspondence with Claudel).

'Notes on a Possible Generalisation of the Theories of Freud' in *The Criterion*, Vol. I. No. 4. July, 1923. (Translation of the study of Freud published in *Quelques progrès dans l'étude du coeur humain.*)

BIBLIOGRAPHICAL WORKS

Charlot, Pierre, *Jacques Rivière*, Une Vie Ardente et sincère, Bloud et Gay, n.d. [1934].

Claudel, P. and Gide, A., *Correspondance 1899-1926*, Gallimard, 1949.

Du Bos, Charles, *Approximations*, 2ième série, Crès, 1927.

Extraits d'un journal 1908-1928, Éditions de la Pléiade, 1929.

Journal 1921-1928, 4 Vols, Corrêa, 1946-1950.

Gide, André, *Incidences* Gallimard, 1924.

Journal 1889-1939 (Bibliothèque de la Pléiade), Gallimard, 1939.

Jans, Adrien, *La Pensée de Jacques Rivière* (Collection: 'Essais et Portraits'), Brussels: Éditions de la Cité Chrétienne, 1938.

Magny, Claude-Edmonde, *Histoire du roman français depuis 1918*, (Collection: 'Pierres Vives'), I, Éditions du Seuil, 1950.

Massis, Henri, *Jugements*, II, Plon, 1924.

Mauriac, François, *Le Tourment de Jacques Rivière*, Strasbourg: Éditions de la Nuée-Bleue, 1926.

(Contains 'Anima Naturaliter Christiana' and a review of *A la Trace de Dieu*).

Du Côté de chez Proust, La Table Ronde, 1947.

(Reprint of the material from *Le Tourment de Jacques Rivière* with fresh material on Rivière as well as a study of Proust.)

Rivière, Isabelle, *Le Bouquet de roses rouges*, Corrêa, 1935.

La Guérison, Corrêa, 1936.

Roos, Elisabeth Geertruida de, *Het Essayistisch Werk van Jacques Rivière*, Amsterdam: H. J. Paris, 1931.

Schlumberger, Jean, *Éveils*, Gallimard, 1950.

Various writers, *Hommage à Jacques Rivière*, special number of *La Nouvelle Revue Française*, No. 139, April, 1925. (Contains *inter alia* a full bibliography up to 1925 including articles in journals which have not yet been reprinted, 'Extraits d'un Journal de Captivité' and letters to André Gide 1909-1913. The account of Rivière's last days by Jacques Copeau is of particular interest).